PRENTICE HALL
FOUNDATIONS OF MODERN SOCIOLOGY SERIES

Alex Inkeles, Editor

A
SOCIOLOGICAL
PERSPECTIVE
ON POLITICS

A SOCIOLOGICAL PERSPECTIVE ON POLITICS

MILDRED A. SCHWARTZ

Department of Sociology
University of Illinois at Chicago

Prentice Hall, Englewood Cliffs, New Jersey 07632

Library of Congress Cataloging-in-Publication Data

Schwartz, Mildred A.
    A sociological perspective on politics / Mildred A. Schwartz.
      p.   cm. -- (Prentice-Hall foundations of modern sociology
  series)
    Includes index.
    ISBN 0-13-821133-7
    1. Political sociology.   I. Title.   II. Series.
  JA76.S365 1990
  306'.2--dc20   89-8377
                                                               CIP

Editorial/production supervision: Betsy Keefer
Manufacturing buyer: Peter Havens

 © 1990 by Prentice-Hall, Inc.
A Division of Simon & Schuster
Englewood Cliffs, New Jersey 07632

Printed in the United States of America
10 9 8 7 6 5 4 3 2

ISBN 0-13-821133-7

Prentice-Hall International (UK) Limited, *London*
Prentice-Hall of Australia Pty. Limited, *Sydney*
Prentice-Hall Canada, Inc., *Toronto*
Prentice-Hall Hispanoamericana, S.A., *Mexico*
Prentice-Hall of India Private Limited, *New Delhi*
Prentice-Hall of Japan, Inc., *Tokyo*
Simon & Schuster Asia Pte. Ltd., *Singapore*
Editora Prentice-Hall do Brasil, Ltda., *Rio de Janeiro*

CONTENTS

A
SOCIOLOGICAL
PERSPECTIVE
ON POLITICS

CHAPTER 1

POLITICS AND EVERYDAY LIFE

SOCIAL EXPERIENCE OF POLITICS

Politics at the University

Patient observation of chimpanzees at the Darmstadt Zoo revealed a complex world of shifting coalitions, headed by leaders that emerged, grew weak, and were superceded, and clear differences between the sexes in their ties to coalitions. It seems fitting that ethologist Frans DeWaal (1982) should call the results of his research *Chimpanzee Politics*. Some readers of that volume were quick to relate the behavior of individual chimpanzees to human counterparts. We need not indulge in such romantic comparisons to recognize a more profound truth in DeWaal's observations—politics is a part of all continuing social experiences.

Another who recognized the pervasiveness of politics was an unhappy student at the University of Illinois at Chicago. She had written on a washroom wall, "I hate this university—everything here is political." When I asked my students to interpret this, they responded with diverse meanings. According to Paul Bauch, "She equates politics with something undesirable. She saw the bureaucracy as a barrier between her and her goals. The statement seems to be an outcry to release her frustration and her feeling of powerlessness." Marilyn Ware thought it was related to whom you know and the particular demands of individual professors—"to get information and opportunities depends on your ability to get the right person to like you enough to let you into the system or through the red tape." Stanley Snarskis suggested that the graffito might reflect the feeling that "she had no control over her destiny and no power over her choices. It is very hard to get little things accomplished here." Alfreda Braun

1

thought the student "was unable to accomplish simple things like obtaining records, financial aid, or information in general through the system. She probably had problems getting attention from staff. The university probably seems impersonal." To Christina Hansen, "The university is a place where a student is impotent in the face of a huge, disordered, and hierarchical structure." Vincent Price took a broader view, considering the university as "just a reflection of the larger social system; success or failure is already prescribed and beyond the control of the individual."

Politics and Society

The unknown student's diatribe against the university and my own students' interpretations of it demonstrate those qualities of politics that are experienced and understood by virtually everyone. Students' language may not have been precise, but even at the very outset of their course, political elements in relations between students and the university were already apparent to them. Students perceived at least four ways in which politics enters everyday life in the university: through involvement in relations of *power,* in which participants are of unequal strength; by presence in an *organization,* where the division of labor is associated with differences in power; through involvement in relations that reveal tensions and conflict between the *goals* of individuals and groups within the organization; by presence in a particular kind of organization (the university) with the capacity to create and confirm status differences associated with power differences and accepted as *legitimate* in the larger society.

What the students observed can be generalized even further to note that any stable social relationship encounters political problems and uses political processes to deal with them. The need to set collective goals and to ensure the distribution of valued resources is as likely to take place in the family as in a state; uses of power and legitimated authority are as common to parents as to government. To illustrate the generality of politics, we will move between the microdetails of politics in the university and the macroscopic interplay between society and state, noting common elements and essential differences.

Politics arises from a collectivity's experiences with the uneven distribution of socially valued resources and the pressures those experiences create for responsive decisions and actions. Relevant responses are those that seek to foster, mitigate, or replace existing inequalities. This neutral wording cloaks intense conflicts over why there is uneven distribution, what is valued, or who are the beneficiaries of responsive actions. Such conflicts will be elaborated in later chapters; here they will be given brief attention, emphasizing the universal political problems in making choices about scarce resources.

The structures within which political problems arise are tied to the forms problems take and to the ways in which they are dealt with. Like political problems, social organization will concern us in later chapters, whether taking form in the complexity of the state, the elaborate bureaucracy of a university, the committed fellowship of a social movement, or the intimacy of a small group. In this chapter, our coverage of social organization will be restricted to those elements that are necessary as initial tools.

In describing the basic building blocks for a sociology of politics, we begin with the processes of power and legitimacy.

SOURCES OF POWER

Power Defined

The perspective adopted in this volume is that power pervades all social arrangements. It agrees with Hawley's (1963, 422) thesis: "Every social act is an exercise of power, every social relationship is a power equation, and every social group or system is an organization of power." Max Weber's (1978, I, 52) widely used definition of power as "the probability that one actor within a social relationship will be in a position to carry out his own will despite resistance" allows us to identify when power is exercised,[1] although it would then be misleading to conceptualize power as the act of an individual. We are dealing with a social world in which "power is the property of the social relation; it is not an attribute of the actor" (Richard Emerson, 1962, 31).

Negative Sanctions

Any power relation ultimately rests on the possibility of using force. Weber (1978, II, 904) described the state as unique in its monopoly over the legitimate use of force, although the creation of the state does not deny the appropriateness of force to other social units. A parent may physically punish a child without violating the state's monopoly. Yet the fact that a parent can be prosecuted for abuse of his or her own child signifies the limits on using force set by the state.

Tilly's historical survey of rebellions and revolutions led him to conclude that it is violence that is the most commonly exercised form of power coming from the state (Tilly, 1978, 177). Yet it can also be argued that the too frequent use of severe sanctions will actually deplete the power of those who use them. Once force is used, the worst has been done—if it is ineffective, there are no alternatives (Collins, 1982, 68). From the position of those who use power, it is better—that is, less costly—to instill fear in opponents and potential deviants than to actually spend resources in punishing them.

For the most part, the university's most important negative sanction is the ability to exclude people—as students, faculty, or staff—either from initial entry or from continued presence. This ability to exclude deviants is, in general, often the most severe form of punishment available to any group or organization, whether made up of family members, friends, workers, or citizens. Here too control is achieved through fear of sanctions. As my students recognized, the fear of failing tests and exams is an effective check for those who want to remain in the university.

The effectiveness of threatened exclusion as a means of controlling opponents and dissidents is premised on the human desire to be part of social groups; ultimately, it is a condition of survival. Those who want to be part of a group are then vulnerable to its power. The workers engaged in wiring and soldering circuits at the Hawthorn plant of the Western Electric Company had developed their own norms for what constituted a fair day's work (Roethlisberger and Dickson, 1939). They could enforce these norms on each other by informal social controls, including the practice of "binging"—playfully hitting each other, often painfully—a sanction that approximates the use of force. One worker, however, refused to go along with the group's norms despite his exclusion from the friendly banter at work and social contacts after work, or the frequency with which he was the object of binging. The others had nothing further they could do, since management had not accepted their work norms as the official ones. Being an integrated member of the bank-wiring workroom was less important to the deviant worker than taking home a larger paycheck.

In the university, Ms. Ware spoke of the importance of getting along with others in order to avoid negative sanctions. This observation may be true, but as long as there is no extremely deviant behavior of the kind that arouses automatic removal, it is still possible to graduate from the university without conforming either to faculty or to other students' expectations of what makes a good student, just as it was possible to remain working at the Hawthorn plant without conforming to either management or other workers' norms.

Institutionalization

Power can be used in more predictable ways when the norms supported by informal social control sanctions are incorporated into regulations or rules of conduct. The inability of the bank-wiring-room workers to achieve full consensus rested on their inability to make their norms the official ones. In contrast, in work settings like those studied by Crozier (1964), where workers are organized into trade unions, norms that were developed about work loads and seniority could be used in negotiations with management. Trade union power is demonstrated whenever worker norms become part of the formal work rules.

Much of the time neither force, exclusion, nor informal means of social control like gossip are needed in order for power to be exercised. This is because power can emerge and be sustained simply through the absence of opposition. Collins (1982, 72–75) explains this phenomenon by the individual inclination to take things for granted because of the limits of human cognition. J. D. Wright (1976) offers support for this generalization from his examination of survey data, collected to determine why there was not greater political participation by the ordinary citizen. He found some who felt current political arrangement and leaders were satisfactory; others who thought they were not ideal, but could still be worse; and still others who, while not totally satisfied, saw no alternative. The end result of all such views is a reservoir of largely uncomplaining acquiescence with the status quo. Using later data, from the 1970s, Hamilton and Wright (1986, 327–373) again confirmed low levels of concern with political issues and, even though there had been rising dissatisfaction with government performance, the absence of a buildup of protest.

Acquiescence at the individual level is not, in fact, a source of power. What acquiescence does is offer an arena of operation devoid of challenge to those who already have power. Under such circumstances, one may wonder whether existing power relations could ever be changed. In theories of systemic power, in which political arrangements and distributions of power are perceived as having a life and momentum of their own because they reflect dominant economic interests, the former are perceived as difficult to dislodge (Alford and Friedland, 1975, 450). For example, Alford (1975) offers an explanation of why the delivery of health services in New York state was not geared to the interests of the consumer by arguing that the high status of the medical profession led to the latter's interests dominating to such an extent that, even without active intervention, others in government and in the hospitals were prepared to act on the profession's behalf. Similarly, Stone (1980) relates decisions made at the community level to the system of stratification; that is, decision-makers keep in mind the presumed interests of the dominant business community.

Student references to the "system" were also premised on a view of the university, as well as the larger society of which it is a part, as more or less permanent structures of relations. For the student to penetrate that system was extremely difficult, yet he or she had to do so in order to be judged successful. Students did not question how the "system" had taken shape, revealing their innocence of such ideological debates as Althusser's (1969) interpretation of Marx, that the mode of production in a society determines which relations will become dominant.

A counterpart of conceptions of systemic power based on group dominance consists of those that attribute power to the symbolic order and the ways this order is manifested in language and social relations generally. So Cancian (1985, 253–264) states that love has been feminized in American society, implying that the qualities it entails are appropriate only for women. This tendency, she argues, ensures that in competitive situations, such as those found in the workplace, women's styles of cooperation will contribute to their subordinate status. This kind of perspective once again leaves us in a world largely impenetrable to change.

Control over Resources

Theories that recognize a more changeable world see in uncertainty the circumstances for giving access to power. Power as the means to control uncertainty may lie outside formal definitions of who is in charge yet still be highly significant. For example, in a highly mechanized factory, where activities are routinized, virtually the only area of uncertainty that may arise is when machines break down. As Crozier (1964) observed in a monopolistic tobacco factory, machinery repairs were outside the routine, as were the mechanics who did them. Protected by the absence of written repair manuals, mechanics had power to affect the work process according to when they did repairs or how long they took. In the university setting, analogous control over uncertainty may be exerted by staff and service personnel, who decide what information can be provided or how long it will take to process requests. This form of power is never possible for students and rare for faculty.

Access to information and position in a communication system are themselves sources of power, in a sense explicating how uncertainty can be reduced. From their own exposure to the unyielding procedures of a large state university, students were acutely aware of how lack of information could be troublesome. They empathized with accounts of frustration arising from not knowing where to turn for help or how to respond to what looked like capricious hurdles. Karen Lange thought that the student who had vented her feelings on the washroom wall had perhaps "tried to get a credit check performed in less than twelve weeks, which would be a miracle in itself."

Collins's (1982, 63) view that money is one source of power gives a modified contemporary expression to the Marxist perspective that, under capitalism, all relations are reduced to monetary ones (Marx, 1971, 59–64). My students, however, were much closer to Max Weber's (1978, II, 926–939) analysis, separating power from wealth and reputation as three sources of stratification operating in three different spheres of life—the political, economic, and social. While wealth and status can be used to acquire power, and the three are frequently correlated, each needs to be understood as part of a separate domain. These distinctions are not simply analytical ones but shape everyday expectations, as exemplified by the irritation of 15 "ordinary" men—that is, white, mainly blue collar, with no more than high school education, living in a middle-sized city—with the role of trade unions, even though almost all were union members. Their discomfort could be understood as an imbalance in their perceptions of the power of unions (relatively great) and the latter's social status (relatively low) (Lane, 1962, 132–135). Such an imbalance might be even greater now, because, when the study was done in the late 1950s, unions enjoyed even higher prestige than they do today (Lipset and Schneider, 1983, 39–40), when there is increased concern about the excessive power of "big" unions (Lipset and Schneider, 1983, 206–209).

The distinctions among criteria of stratification recognized by students were a measure of the university's moral integrity, in which academic qualifications are the basis of faculty hiring and promotion and student admission and advancement. Students did not expect the university's power to be affected by the wealth or status of university trustees, donors, alumni, or students. Yet power also had its poignant side, in ways analogous to the ambivalence of Lane's subjects about trade unions. Karl Marx might have called their reactions "false consciousness" (see Chapter 3), but, as far as the students were concerned, they were closer to Groucho Marx, when he said that he would not be caught dead in any club that would admit him as a member. For many students from ethnic, working-class backgrounds, often the first in their family to attend college, acknowledgement of their own relatively low financial position and social status was only confirmed by attendance at a starkly modern but unkempt campus whose prestige is distinctly lower than the prominent private universities in the area or its older sister campus downstate.

Power as it is used here pervades all social relations and arises from multiple sources (Wrong, 1980). While power is a basic political process, it is not the whole of politics. Before moving to the definitive problems and related social structures, there is one other process that needs consideration—the process of legitimation.

LEGITIMATE AUTHORITY

Bases of Legitimacy

Everyone would agree that an armed robber has power over those he robs because of his ability to induce others to hand over their money, presumably against their will. But do we similarly agree that an armed robbery is a political act? Some armed robberies are—when they are explicitly linked with the politics of groups like the Posse Comitatus, a radical antitax group that has operated against established authorities in the western United States, or the Symbionese Liberation Army, a now defunct radical group in California that intended to use the proceeds of its robberies to take over the government. What makes the ordinary robbery immediately unpolitical is its lack of legitimacy. This is more than simply being an illegal act. The operation of a principle of legitimacy allows governments to levy taxes and citizens to pay them; cities to require that motorists stop at red lights and motorists to comply or face the threat of punishment; parents to care for their own children and the state to interfere when there is noticeable neglect; children to be required to attend school and to do so in fact; professors to demand the writing of papers and exams and students to hand them in on time. The fact that none of my students mentioned the importance of rules governing relations in the university or the appropriateness of demands placed on students to take exams, write papers, and so on did not mean that they did not understand that a principle of legitimacy was operating. More likely they were avoiding mention of the kinds of constraints that no one likes, no matter how much we agree that they are a necessary part of life. Yet students certainly understood how graduating from the university would supply them with credentials that would legitimate subsequent claims to status.

The significance that sociologists attach to legitimacy derives mainly from the work of Max Weber, who taught us that legitimacy was not a monolithic quality but one that was situationally and historically determined. Weber (1978, I, 215–216) did this by showing how legitimacy may arise from three different sources. The first is *tradition,* where custom determines what is considered legitimate. The prototypic traditional ruler is a hereditary monarch. Traditional authority is typically found in nonindustrial, relatively uncomplex societies, but it never totally loses importance, because custom offers a form of continuity and a context for appropriate behavior that is quickly grasped and easily communicated. In the family, the authority of parents over children is a primitive social bond resistant to encroachment from other kinds of authority. In the university, tradition has been found in the operation of ascribed characteristics where students, to whom the relevance of graduation from an Ivy League college or publications in major scholarly journals may not be visible, look for authority in cues of age and sex. Queasy new assistant professors then grow beards or mustaches, if they are male, or don glasses and business suits, if they are female, in efforts to convey their claim to professorial status.

Rational-legal bases of authority are found only in those societies where there is a system of written record keeping and a money economy. Authority derives from written rules and regulations and belongs to those who demonstrate their technical qualifications for the position. Strictly speaking, authority goes with the position, not the individual who happens to be occupying it. The prototype of rational legal authority is the bureaucratic officeholder. Even though professors may complain about bureaucrats, they display a common claim to authority when they are hired and promoted on the basis of specified technical qualifications.

Unlike the limitations on traditional and rational-legal authority, the third basis of authority may arise in any kind of society. It comes from *charisma,* a concept from the Greek used in Christian theology to signify the "gift of grace." Today we are accustomed to hearing virtually any popular Hollywood actor or politician described as charismatic. We are better off, however, sticking with Weber's definition of an extraordinary quality, giving its possessor the authority to propose revolutionary changes. A true charismatic figure does not ask for support on the basis of tradition or existing rules and regulations but rather because of his or her personal ability to bring about change. The prototypic charismatic leader is the founder of a new social or political movement.

Weber (1978, I, 267) would have sympathized with our propensity to apply charisma more broadly than his definition specified, especially in the realm of politics. He recognized that politicians, to be elected, had to draw on both traditional and rational-legal sources of authority and might even make quasi-charismatic appeals based on their special abilities to solve problems. But I find it most useful to confine charismatic *authority* to what can be found in new and revolutionary situations and to then refer to the charismatic *qualities* of those extraordinary political figures who come from a traditional or rational-legal system but still make their own special appeal. If Martin Luther King is considered a charismatic leader, President John F. Kennedy was one with charismatic qualities.

This way of talking about charismatic authority may suggest that legitimacy lies with the individual leader. Yet I. L. Horowitz (1966), confronting the widespread existence of single-party systems in the Third World, generally as the heirs of movements of national liberation, considers it appropriate to speak of "party charisma."

> The single party assumes the "god-like" features of leadership, which in the medieval world belonged to a series of Popes, in the seventeenth and eighteenth centuries belonged to a series of monarchs—some enlightened, but all absolute—and which, in

the present century, have been raised to a new level by such secular rulers as Hitler, Stalin, and, on a lesser level, Mussolini and Perón. (I. L. Horowitz, 1966, 227)

Horowitz alerts us to the fact that, just as rational-legal and traditional authority rests on institutionalized foundations, so too does charisma have an institutional context, even though initially it is one that has to be built. Legitimacy does not simply refer to a set of attitudes that a person is "right" for a position. Nor does it merely refer to the right of an individual or group to give orders and make decisions. A principle of legitimacy is a transactional relation between leaders and led, between institutions and their normative support (Richard Emerson, 1962). On the one hand, it presumes that those affected by the authority are willing to be bound by its actions, whether they like them or not. On the other hand, it presumes that those seeking or exercising authority will agree to accept the responsibilities that go with it. Put this way, it may again suggest an individualistic flavor to legitimacy by stressing the relation between leaders and followers. On the contrary, legitimation requires an institutional setting, a normative order.

Legitimacy does not refer to goodness or even to legality, as is evident when we speak of the legitimacy of a charismatic leader who may well be challenging an existing legal system. Regardless of its source, legitimacy establishes the rightful place of leaders and institutions in a system of authority. It is in this sense that political legitimacy parallels what is meant by the legitimacy of children—the establishment of their rightful place in a kinship system.

Sources of Instability

The transactional qualities of legitimacy can be even better understood once we recognize that they are not fixed. Weber gives us insight into sources of change by treating the ways in which each basis of authority holds the seeds of its own delegitimation. The most familiar of these is the relative instability of charismatic authority (Weber, 1978, II, 1121–1148). Without the backing of either tradition or the legal system, the charismatic leader who fails to demonstrate his or her special gifts may quickly be left without the confirming capacity of a following. In addition, charisma is often routinized by the demands of everyday existence, when its revolutionary quality becomes subordinated to such mundane responsibilities as organizing meetings, providing shelter to followers, or handling a payroll. Kelley and Klein (1986) hypothesize that even those radical revolutions aimed at destroying an existing system of stratification often produce comparable systems, as people with the requisite skills find new job opportunities in what were initially movements propelled by the enthusiasm of their followers. A charismatic figure like Dr. Eric Williams of Trinidad could help lead his country to independence, but once independence was gained, his liberation movement became a political party, the People's National Movement (PNM), and acquired the responsibilities of governing. The PNM did govern, under Williams's guidance, by acting in a reformist, rather than a revolutionary, manner (Oxaal, 1968).

Not even the weight of tradition can protect legitimacy in all circumstances. An heir apparent who is defective, an ambitious second wife with aspirations for her offspring, an unprecedented disaster that places the society in crisis—all are circumstances when the customary ways of defining authority can be challenged. In the history of Europe, for example, the limitations of traditional rulers or their heirs opened opportunities for new forms of authority. In 18th-century England, the physical or mental disabilities of George III allowed Parliament to acquire new powers, and in 20th-century Russia, the hemophilia of the eldest son contributed to the weakening of the monarchy. Huntington (1968, 177–191) argues that traditional monarchies in the last half of this century faced the dilemma of adapting to economic and social changes by centralizing power and thus putting their own survival in question because traditional rule and centralization are organizationally incompatible.

What about the authority associated with rational-legal systems? Is it immune from such challenges? On the one hand, the "iron cage" of bureaucracy that Weber described seemed insulated from the kinds of instability that are associated with either tradition or charisma. Others, emphasizing the negative connotations of bureaucracy—its red tape, inflexibility, and apparent unresponsiveness to change—perceive inherent instabilities to be present in bureaucracies as well. Alvin Gouldner's analysis of a wildcat strike at a gypsum plant illustrates both how a factory bureaucracy functions by adapting to the personal strengths and weaknesses of participants and how a disruption of these routinized patterns provokes a breakdown of the system. Under Doug, the previous foreman, concessions had been made to workers' absenteeism or personal use of plant materials. With a new foreman, Vince, informal arrangements no longer operated and workers recalled probably exaggerated descriptions of their earlier experiences. "Doug *trusted* his men to do a job. Vincent doesn't. Doug didn't come around so much. He *relied* on the men" (Gouldner, 1954, 87). Whatever the reality of such judgments, the tensions that provoked them were real. They represented a challenge to authority that would be increased when Vincent too was abruptly replaced, contributing to conditions that led to a worker walkout.

Gouldner's example supports Lipset's (1981, 65) position that any crisis of change, frequently generated by a change in leadership, provides the setting for a crisis of legitimacy. In the United States, just as in other countries, we often speak of a honeymoon period for newly elected leaders, but that time can also be perceived as crisis-prone. It is surely no accident that what is known as the Cuban missile crisis occurred shortly after President Kennedy was elected, when the Soviet leaders attempted to install intercontinental ballistic missiles on Cuba that could have reached as far as Washington (Allison, 1971). At that time President Kennedy was untried, and the Soviets saw an opportunity for testing him. If he had failed the test, the potential for a crisis of legitimacy was already there.

Lipset's (1981, 64) distinction between the effectiveness of a state—its "actual performance, the extent to which the system satisfies the basic functions of government"—and its legitimacy allows him to illustrate how a decline in effectiveness tends to undermine legitimacy. According to Habermas (1975, 68–75), the capitalist state is especially prone to crises of legitimacy because of its expanding role, but such crises can be deflected where there is a highly supportive value system. In contrast, legitimacy of authority and the organizations it sustains is undermined by intense and prolonged conflict, especially over religious issues or the admission of new groups into the political arena. As a result of such conflict in places like present-day Lebanon or Northern Ireland, even the continuity of the state is open to question.

Universities too have their crises of legitimacy for both intrinsic and extrinsic reasons. In Latin American countries, especially in periods of political suppression, universities provide some shelter to those who want to challenge the system, but they may also reap the consequences of having done so by restrictions or shutdown (Albornoz, 1966, 250–256). During the 1950s, activist students played a role in the overthrow of Perón in Argentina and Pérez Jiménez in Venezuela. Under communism, Chinese universities have been the setting for legitimizing the privileged status of new groups—the children of workers and farmers—and disputing the claims of others—the old middle class and professionals. But they have also been the arena for challenging the government, as 1986 student riots in Shanghai revealed. The expansion of the student population in the 1960s—a result of the baby boom following World War II—shook the authority of the university in many western countries; one reason was clearly the strain so many new students placed on facilities and operations. Coming at a time when a youth culture was experimenting with its own kinds of music, dress, and interpersonal relations, the traditions of most universities were not sufficiently strong to withstand assault (Lipset, 1976). In France, for example, not only were universities forced to expand their number to accommodate increased enrollment, but the disruptions that occurred in them spilled over to affect other parts of civil society, including the state (Touraine, 1971).

From examples such as these we can conclude that legitimacy is a critical component in stabilizing political relations. Yet it also has volatile qualities, most likely to emerge when the structure of relations it otherwise protects is not able to meet changing circumstances.

POLITICAL PROBLEMS

The Substance of Politics

The essence of politics is its purpose—the right to define what is socially valuable and to make the decisions about how what is valuable should be distributed. Aristotle (1962, 25), although confining politics to the state, captured the purposeful nature of politics generally by his statement that ''Every state is an association of persons formed with a view to some good.'' Similarly, although from a more individualistic perspective, social purpose is evident in Lasswell's (1958) definition of politics as ''who gets what, when, how.'' Politics implies inequality in resources, leading to differences in the ability to control or be controlled. Decisions concerning the allocation of resources will be binding on the collectivity as a whole; to ensure that they are accepted as binding, power may be exerted, but ideally under conditions in which legitimacy is acknowledged. It is the existence of inequalities, whose roots are discussed in Chapter 2, that create political problems in every social setting where they are found. How political problems are then met depends on the mobilization of affected interests and the resources they can command, the subjects of Chapter 3.

None of my students expressly stated that politics meant the capacity to define and regulate inequalities. Yet they still conveyed an unspoken recognition of this meaning from their agreement to remain students, despite evident dissatisfaction with the organization of the university and the way power is distributed within it, because the university controls desired resources and provides access to future ones. They saw the university as a place for forming friendships, meeting potential mates, and acquiring a ticket to a good job, all on the road to social mobility. While Mr. Price was clearest in seeing the role of the university as a reflection of the goals of the larger society, and most cynical about the opportunity for mobility it will provide, he was still unusually aware of how a university degree would enhance his chances for election to future political office.

This conception of the universality of political problems does not confine problems to the state but finds them as well in family life, work organization, informal groups, and voluntary associations. We can even speak of the political life of a criminal gang because it has its own goals, its own access to and use of power, and its own legitimacy. The latter remains unstable, to be sure, because it is constantly under attack from other groups, but it still has a reality for its members.

Political Values

Politics rests on beliefs and values about how a social system does and should work. In any social setting, we can expect variations in those beliefs and values, just as we can expect that some will dominate because they are associated with individuals and groups who are themselves dominant. To the extent that values determine collective goals, the former may create a world view for those that adhere to them—in other words, an ideology. The role that ideologies play in the political sphere, including the shape they may give to the state, is discussed in Chapter 4.

ORGANIZATION

Defining Bureaucracy

Politics is most often associated with the state and its specialized organs of government, treated in Chapter 5. More fundamentally, it is possible to see the polity as "first of all (both historically and theoretically) an organization" (Collins,

1968, 49). And, as the comments of my students illustrated, it is also easy to see bureaucracy generally as a self-contained political system. While a bureaucracy may be thought of, in positive or at least neutral terms, as a complex organization for efficiently achieving some goals, students are hardly unique in describing and experiencing its negative qualities. Unwieldy size, red tape, impersonality, and unresponsiveness have become standard criticisms of bureaucracy. According to Ms. Ware, the only way a student can get through the barriers in the university is to know the right person, who will serve as a guide in what Ms. Hansen called ''the bureaucratic disorder.''

Following the lead of Max Weber (1978, I, 217–226), a nonevaluative definition of bureaucracy emphasizes its rational character. This entails a hierarchy of authority based on jobs filled through technical qualifications, in which jobs are separated from the personal qualities of those who carry them out by adherence to formal rules and regulations. What is political about such an organization is its character as a system of authority—its provision of a structure of relations for making binding decisions on behalf of the organization. The Weberian definition of bureaucracy has been modified by those who emphasize either natural- or open-systems models of organization, but, regardless of the primary emphasis, politics remains at the core. For example, open-system theorists like Cyert and March (1963) or Pfeffer and Salancik (1978) see the operation of organizations in terms of shifting coalitions of competing interests. Where competition is the key process, power is a necessary resource and politics a natural outcome. Natural-system theorists as diverse as Parsons (1960) and Selznick (1949), by emphasizing the survival goals of organizations, draw attention to the political problems of controlling resources.

Varieties of Organization

To say that politics takes place in an organizational context does not mean that it is always a bureaucratic one, even in the modified forms suggested by natural and open systems. One alternative is the kind of organization found in a political movement. Some movements avoid hierarchy by refusing to recognize differences in authority or competence. They may do so by requiring equal participation from adherents recruited not on the basis of technical qualifications but through their commitment to the movement's goals. Because wholehearted commitment also means that a person's life is totally bound up with the movement, there is nothing analogous to the separation of the job from the person found in a bureaucracy. Family, job, friends are all given second place and even shunned if they too are not part of the movement.

In the politics of everyday life, organization may be no more than what is found in an informal group, like a friendship group. Alternatively, it could be the elaborate but relatively unique form of social organization found in the nuclear family. Whatever the size or form, however, it is the fact of organization that provides political meaning because it always implies some collective experience.

Organization of whatever form is so important for politics that it is given special attention in Chapter 3.

PLAN OF THE BOOK

Summary

Power is a principal political process but is not, in itself, sufficient to define the nature of politics. This is true because power is such a pervasive means of the strong controlling the weak when strength can range from force to information. Additional specification of fundamental political processes is provided by the importance of legitimate authority. The basic nature of power and legitimacy merit their lengthy treatment here, leaving the remainder of this text for elaboration of the other topics raised in this chapter.

Politics requires organization to create a political system, ranging from the miniature polity found through the continuing relationships of small groups to the grand scale of the state itself. By basing this volume on the politics of everyday life, I deliberately extend the scope of political relationships into all spheres of life, encompassing all forms of social organization. Organization supplies the context in which political problems arise and are dealt with. The problems at the heart of politics come from the experience of inequalities that demand collectively binding solutions.

Outline

The remainder of this volume offers a brief treatment of major themes in a sociology of politics. There is no attempt to give either a thorough review of the literature or a comprehensive coverage of all topics that might be of concern to sociologists. My selection of themes has been guided by a desire to present a coherent set of topics culled from the literature that experience in the classroom has revealed to be both interesting and useful in understanding the political world. Illustrations draw on a range of historical periods and national settings against which to compare experiences in the United States. The relation between the theoretical bases of the topics selected and the ways they take shape in individual and group experience is highlighted by emphasizing their relevance to everyday life, generally in the conclusion to each chapter.

The social context out of which power differences arise is examined in Chapter 2 through the lines of cleavage that divide a society. Cleavages are then related to political alignments, and the special circumstances of the United States are examined separately.

The theme of cleavages and their political expression is further explored in Chapter 3 in terms of how the former are mobilized. Variations in the conditions that foster mobilization and differences in the opportunities available to particular cleavage groups are first examined in historical perspective and then used to account for the absence of a strong socialist movement in the United States. This chapter emphasizes the importance of organization for successful mobilization as a prelude to evaluating the effects of mobilization itself.

The ways in which political issues and events are given meaning are the subject of Chapter 4. Reasons for uneasiness in the face of ideological thinking are first put to rest by distinguishing between ''grand ideologies'' and less formal and comprehensive meaning systems. How ideologies are diffused and what impact they have make up the conclusion of the chapter.

This volume concludes by addressing sociological concern with the role of the state, emphasizing the importance of state autonomy and historical specificity. Anglo-American experiences with the state are sufficiently unique to lead social scientists to focus on the study of local government in Britain and local community power in the United States. Commonly discussed dissatisfactions with the role of the state arise either when it is seen in a crisis stage or its policy-making outcomes are considered deficient.

NOTE

1.   Weber's use of probability is not what is now meant by this concept and can be disregarded.

CHAPTER 2

SOCIAL CLEAVAGES AND POLITICAL ALIGNMENTS

INTRODUCTION

Inequalities that grow from differences among categories of people create the political world. Not all differences lead to inequalities, nor are they necessarily of the same kind, even when they do, but all socially recognized differences have the potential to affect access to resources and rewards. Since politics is our concern, and not inequalities in themselves, we need to determine the circumstances when unequal resource distribution becomes associated with competing interests. In this chapter the focus is on those aspects of resource distribution that are societal in scope. Because they permit the social location of virtually everyone, they provide the link between society and everyday life. The connection between social aggregates and political alignments comes about through the transformation of the social aggregates into collective actors. The historical process is illustrated in this chapter with examples from Western Europe and the United States.

The existence of stable political alignments also raises the possibility of change or realignment. Sources of change in group politics are found in historical circumstances, the experiences of aligned groups, channels of political expression, and the mobilization of new groups. The last leads us into Chapter 3, on mobilization.

Once again we find in the details of university experiences ways of illustrating political divisions and processes. In the United States existing cleavages and changing social conditions are made manifest in the university. Like education in general (Marshall, 1964, 89), the university plays a bridging role between cleavages and alignments by enabling individuals and groups to find their place in the political community.

LINES OF CLEAVAGE

Roots in Kinship

Since politics concerns how what is valued is, and should be, distributed, we need to understand the basis of distribution. If all valued resources were distributed equally and there were no way for some people to get more than others, there would be no political problem. As long as there is competition over what is valued and dispute over who deserves to get most or, at least, more of what is valued, then there are grounds for the emergence of competing interests. These potentially competing interests are defined as social cleavages, divisions, or "fault lines" (Lane, 1959, 193). They are the major ways of dividing any society in order to capture the principal lines of potential conflict. At this point we can only speak of conflict as "potential" because, as will be developed in Chapter 3, cleavages do not always become the basis of overt conflict.

The most thorough, though still incomplete, analysis of lines of cleavage in Western society has been traced by Lipset and Rokkan (1967, 1–64). I follow their argument by agreeing that the most fundamental source of cleavage is tied to kinship. That is, in all societies (and not just Western ones), the easiest and most universally applicable way of classifying people is in terms of their family relationships. Family, in turn, has a territorial dimension—a customary place of residence. It is the elaboration of what begin as kinship ties, founded on blood or marriage, that later become elaborated in divisions according to race, ethnicity, nationality, language, and religion. The latter all share the characteristic of locating people according to who they are because of birth.

The ways in which nationality or religion can be understood as extensions of kinship are obscured if we think only in terms of the contemporary United States, where both appear to have an almost totally voluntary nature. But from ancient times, religion has been the basis of a primary identity, acquired along with family and tribe or synonymous with them. Even the concept of Christianity as a voluntarily acquired faith, and the subsequent practice of large-scale conversion of adults, still leaves an important sense in which religion confers a primary identity that is similar to other kinship-based ones, by providing a marriage pool and a kind of extended family.

The process by which immigrants to the United States become citizens may also conceal how nationality is more usually a birthright that can only be abrogated by the death of the one who holds it. The contemporary recognition of territorial national identity in Western society remains strongest in Switzerland, where rights of citizenship are linked to the commune of one's family's origin, regardless of present residence or even birthplace.

Lipset and Rokkan argue that, in the Western world, the struggles for national identity and liberation from the rule of supranational powers or from related church privileges were fought in the 17th and 18th centuries. To the extent that these struggles were won, it was assumed that kinship-related cleavages would subside in political importance.

Work

The second basic way of classifying people is according to what they do. As long as there is some division of labor, differences in what people do to sustain themselves in food and shelter, and to obtain the means of exchange for them, are also criteria of cleavage. Once we move beyond hunting-and-gathering societies to settled agriculture, if land ownership is not communal, then relations to the land are the basis of cleavage, distinguishing those who own the land from those who work it. The contemporary expression of rural conflicts, where agriculture is part of a world economy, has been surveyed by Paige (1975) in 70 countries, primarily less developed ones. He argues that modes of land tenure affect the kinds of political movements that emerge, with sharecropping and migratory-labor estate systems based on wage-dependent workers contributing to revolutionary situations.

Where the organization of agriculture becomes more complex and, at the same time, industrial production more important, then the principal social divisions are between primary and secondary producers. At the time of the U.S. Civil War, for example, agricultural versus industrial lines of cleavage were reinforced through their distinct geographic location. The result, according to Moore (1966, 115), was the creation of "three quite different forms of society in different parts of the country: the cotton-growing South; the West, a land of free farmers; and the rapidly industrializing Northeast." It was out of these conditions, based on slavery in the South, that civil war erupted (Moore, 1966, 135–141).

Over time, the Industrial Revolution that had begun early in the 19th century made industrially based cleavages dominant in the Western world, separating owners from workers. At least since the time of Karl Marx, the expectation has been that these industrially based cleavages would have the greatest political relevance. That is also the position of Lipset and Rokkan, who see the great political struggles of the 19th and 20th centuries as based on economic divisions.

Biology

Lipset and Rokkan's scheme does not predict the political struggles that emerged in the latter part of the 20th century tied to distinctions of age and sex. Cleavages based on primarily biological differences, with the exception of race, are often not considered fully social ones. It was thought that the political relevance of age and sex would be confined to relatively simple societies. Even so, the organization of the Nyakusa, Bantu-speaking cattle herders and cultivators, into villages based on age-grades (that is, men in the same age category, along with their wives and children) was considered highly unusual (M. Wilson, 1967). How much more likely, then, that biology be superseded under conditions of more complex social organization? In other words, many social scientists, from Marx to Lipset and Rokkan, worked with an evolutionary perspective on social cleavages. They had the sense that there were stages of political development such that, in time, some social cleavages would lose political relevance. The inadequacy of this perspective will be examined when we turn next to the subject of how cleavages may become synonymous with alignments.

ALIGNMENTS

Historical Influences

Cleavages are politically important to the extent that they are linked to more or less consistent political expression, that is, manifested as political alignments. Political alignments occur when a social cleavage produces divisions that line up in opposing interest groups, political movements, or political parties. It is possible to speak of political alignments only when the behavior or identification of political groups remains stable over time.

When there are limited rights of political participation or representation, the relation between cleavages and alignments is necessarily narrow, reflecting only those divisions in the society possessing the right to compete. For example, in the 17th century, when the British Parliament represented only property holders, there were still divisions within it tied to the size of holdings and religion. The latter emerged initially from the Protestant Reformation and became elaborated under the internal factionalism of Protestantism. Cleavages were represented in alignments of Court and Country, the former representing the largest landholders, who were followers of the Church of England and had closest ties to the monarchy. Under the reign of Charles I (1625–49), a version of these incompatible interests became locked in civil war. Alignments were not yet political parties, but they were to become recognizable factions, with the Tories on one side and the Whigs on the other (Hill, 1976). More than a century later, following the Industrial Revolution, the Whigs became the political arm of industrial interests while the Tories remained representative of the landed aristocracy. These alignments too would shift when industrial workers were enfranchised. For one thing, a greatly increased electorate propelled the existing factions into organizing as modern political parties, with the Whigs becoming the Liberal Party and the Tories the Conservative Party. As new groups entered the electorate, both parties competed for their support. But when industrial workers had acquired some political self-consciousness, they too sought their own political arm and found it in the British Labour Party. The latter became a substantial electoral force after World War I in response to social changes, while, from the 1920s, the Liberal Party faded to the status of a minor third party (Butler and Stokes, 1969, 249–263). The interests formerly represented by the Liberals were incorporated, for the most part, into the Conservative Party (McKenzie, 1964).

It was evidence of this kind, repeated in some fashion in other Western European countries, that supported generalizations about developing connections between social cleavages and political alignments. But while the sequence outlined occurred largely in response to changes in economic structure, other, noneconomic divisions could remain politically volatile if the problems associated with them were unresolved. For example, the history of English political and economic domination and its relation to religion has made the situation of Northern Ireland virtually immune to political movements based exclusively on economic interests (Rose, 1971, 275–301). In this century, movements of national liberation aimed at freedom from colonial rule have also been difficult to explain if one relies on either a narrowly Marxist orientation or one that assumes development solely in economic terms (e.g., Frank, 1967; Kay, 1975).

Examples like these demonstrate the importance of historical factors, often unique to particular countries, in perpetuating social cleavages. The time at which emerging groups gain access to power has a strong bearing on the development of loyalty to existing political arrangements or on the search for alternative means of political expression. The British sociologist T. H. Marshall (1964) has developed this theme most imaginatively, arguing that the speed with which workers were given political rights after the Industrial Revolution largely determined the shape of class conflict for generations to come. For example, Lipset (1981, 67) takes the position that barriers to political participation and representation suffered by workers in pre–World War I Germany blocked them from developing loyalty to the state. Workers responded by their willingness to be recruited into radical movements, and the state eventually suffered from its weakened legitimacy.

Even where cleavages appear to lose their political significance, they may become reactivated. For example, ethnic-linguistic conflicts between Flemish and Walloons in Belgium had subsided through the institutionalization of privileges given both groups and by their relative regional segregation. But Flemish and Walloon differences in birth rates and changes in the economic structure of the country after World War II activated old cleavage-related alignments into open conflict (Lorwin, 1966, 171–176). Or consider present-day Sri Lanka, where the combination of a search for a unique cultural identity on the part of the dominant Sinhalese and efforts to curtail the economic achievements of the minority Tamils have fueled the rise of Tamil separatism (Tambiah, 1986).

Biology and Party

One reason that earlier writers may have omitted mention of biologically based cleavages is the absence of viable political parties based on age or sex. Even so, the social significance of these biological attributes has found expression in political movements virtually everywhere in the modern world. For example, in the United States, old people made up the following of the Townsend Movement at its peak of membership (over 3 million) between 1935 and 1941 (Cantril, 1941). The Townsend Plan advocated universal old-age pensions, considered too radical for serious consideration. Yet because of the attention the plan generated, it helped influence the introduction of an alternative, the Social Security Act of 1935 (Derthick, 1979, 193–195). Young people have infused the world of politics worldwide with their more revolutionary potential, notably in the 1960s. At that time, demonstrations by organized youth, often enrolled in colleges and universities, shook political customs and established authority (Gitlin, 1987).

Women have been politically active since the middle of the 19th century in the effort to secure passage of woman suffrage, and in 1916 one component of the women's movement in the United States formed the Woman's Party (O'Neill, 1969, 71–88). But having a party of one's own has not been the most significant attribute of the politicization of sociobiological groups. It is rather their ability to act in a unified way, especially with respect to issues that affect them most directly (Piven, 1985, 278–284).

Emergence in the United States

The early history of the United States, with its small population and limited franchise, did not reveal stable alignments until after the broadening of the franchise and the election of Andrew Jackson to the presidency. Lines would continue to shift until the Civil War, which created alignments of such durability that many would last until the Great Depression of the 1930s, and some even longer, separating Republicans in the North from Democrats in the South. Although the American colonies had been settled by those seeking to escape from the great religious wars of Europe, religion itself was a preeminent source of their own aspirations in the new world. Alexis de Tocqueville, who visited the United States in 1831, was quick to discern the relevance of religion in setting the moral tenor of life (Tocqueville, I, 1945, 44–45). That heritage of moral crusading would be manifest in the Civil War, as it would in later events (Hartz, 1955; Schwartz, 1981). Jensen (1971) argues that, up to the mid-1800s, religion was the primary basis of political alignment in the United States. While the pivotal election of 1896 was fought on economic grounds—a major depression having occurred under the first Democratic president elected since the Civil War—religious issues were also pervasive. By then, the western frontier was coming to a close. The character of immigration was already changing the demographic makeup of the country from a largely northern European Protestant one to one where Catholics were becoming majorities in some cities (e.g., Glazer and Moynihan, 1970, 219–229). It is not clear whether, in fact, the Democrats or Republicans of that period were more anti-Catholic, but Republican presidential candidate William McKinley was astute enough to keep the issue obscured, while the Democratic candidate, William Jennings Bryan, campaigned for prohibition, a symbolically anti-Catholic issue.

To be against drinking was often a covert way of expressing opposition to the presence of Catholics and of foreign-born people, not only in the election of 1896 and earlier, but at least as late as 1932, when the 18th Amendment, prohibiting the manufacture, sale, or consumption of alcoholic beverages, was finally repealed

(Carter, 1956). By the early 1900s, Irish Catholics had gained control of urban political machines, particularly Democratic ones (Jensen, 1971, 297), and the lines of cleavage separating prohibition-leaning Republicans from Democrats were superimposed on economic ones, largely reinforced by the Great Depression. When Lazarsfeld and his associates did their pioneering study of voting behavior in Erie County, Ohio, during the 1940 presidential campaign, the relations between political alignment and social cleavages were sharply defined. Rural residents, Protestants, white-collar workers, and the middle class generally were most likely to vote Republican. Urban residents, Catholics, blue-collar workers, and the working class generally were more likely to vote Democratic. Under the circumstances, and despite the small sample of the United States studied, it is not surprising that the authors concluded, "A person thinks, politically, as he is socially. Social characteristics determine political preference" (Lazarsfeld, Berelson, and Gaudet, 1944, 27). Along with support for the Democratic party by blacks and other minorities, as well as the continuation of southern Democratic loyalty, the political alignments of the United States were set for generations.

When Nie, Verba, and Petrocik (1976) reviewed national surveys of voting behavior from 1952 to 1972, they could still see the outlines of these alignments. Yet along with them were indications of change, most notably a decline in support for the Democrats from white southerners. Change was brought about by in-migration from white voters, accustomed to voting Republican, coupled with new efforts by the Republican Party to organize white voters. As the south became economically more diverse, the Republicans could count on their attraction to upper-income groups. At the same time, native southerners were also turning against the Democratic Party because of its stand on civil rights issues, particularly from 1964 on (Lamis, 1984).

Compared to what is found in most European countries, the history of Catholic support for the Democrats had been something of an anomaly. In Europe, at least until widespread secularization, most Catholics had supported conservative or confessional parties. The reason for the more liberal leanings of Catholics in the United States was a matter not so much of religion but of the economic conditions found at the time of arrival. Coming to the crowded cities of the northeast, immigrants were met by Democratic Party machines, eager to recruit new voters and prepared to help them in ways that the more established Republicans were not. From those experiences, the tie between Catholics and the Democratic Party was set.

The period after World War II saw increased prosperity for many ethnic Catholics, even those still in the working class, as higher incomes allowed them to enjoy the status of consumers. In addition, Cold War hostility to the Soviet Union encouraged a kind of domestic anticommunism that was attractive to Catholics. Even the Catholicism of the notoriously anticommunist Senator Joseph McCarthy was not irrelevant and led many Catholics to see the Republican Party as the stronger bulwark against communism (Lipset and Raab, 1978, 226, 229–232). We should also not discount the importance of the popular appeal of President Dwight Eisenhower compared with that of his opponent, Adlai Stevenson, whose divorce made him vulnerable to a kind of criticism meaningful to devout Catholics. The flow of ethnic Catholic voters to the Republicans was temporarily halted by the candidacy of the first Catholic president, John F. Kennedy (Converse et al., 1961), but after his death, the forces already set in motion resumed. So, by the mid-1970s, there was a noticeable decline in support for the Democratic Party by Catholics, those of southern and eastern European origin, and the working class.

A further change noted by Nie and his associates was the rise in number and importance of those who considered themselves political independents. Those without party identification or loyalties in earlier elections, like the one studied by Lazarsfeld, Berelson, and Gaudet (1944), were generally found to be poorly educated, with little interest in or knowledge of politics. They were, in other words, the opposite of the idealized rational citizen who, while not necessarily tied to any party, carefully considered issues and candidates before making an electoral decision. By the mid-1960s, however, there appeared a new category of political independents, no longer apathetic and generally with above-average education. While apathetic citizens still existed, these new kinds of independents were more likely to participate. Because of their lack of firm party identification, the latter would provide a volatile element in future elections.

CURRENT ALIGNMENTS IN THE UNITED STATES

Moving to Realignment

Findings of the sort reported in the preceding paragraphs have stimulated many political commentators to believe that the United States is undergoing a period of dramatic political realignment. An alignment itself generally refers to the stable, largely homogeneous political focus of a group's identification, behavior, or beliefs. A realignment, however, at least since the concept was introduced by V. O. Key (1955, 1959), usually refers to a shift in party fortunes, such that the once dominant party is replaced by the opposition, leading to a new period of dominance. Used this way, a realignment is a shift in the party system. It should also be possible, consistent with the way alignment is defined, to speak of realignment as a replacement of a group's dominant party loyalty.

In the United States, there have been at least three periods of major party realignment. The first occurred in the 1850s, when the Whig party disappeared at the time of the Republican Party's birth. The second took place around 1896, when an apparently revitalized Democratic Party, able to elect Grover Cleveland president in 1892, was unable to consolidate its gains. As a result, the Republicans won a sweeping victory with President McKinley, establishing their status as the majority party until well into the 1920s. By then Democratic strength was on the upswing and the advent of the Great Depression heralded a move to the Democratic Party that would give it majority status for the next 50 years.

This is only a general outline of party fortunes, but it should be sufficiently representative to convey the sense of what is entailed in realignments. To ask, in the 1980s, whether the United States is going through another major realignment is to ask whether those segments of the population associated with major cleavages have altered their partisan loyalties. What is the evidence?

Numerous studies, using questions on party identification first devised by the Survey Research Center of the University of Michigan, have concluded that there has been a sharp decline in the numbers of voters willing to identify themselves with either party. Respondents are regularly asked: "Generally speaking, do you usually think of yourself as a Republican, a Democrat, an Independent, or what?" If the answer is either Republican or Democrat, then the question is: "Would you call yourself a strong Republican (Democrat) or not a very strong Republican (Democrat)?" Those who answer Independent are asked: "Do you think of yourself as closer to the Republican or Democratic party?" Independents, regardless of party leanings, were 22 percent of the national sample studied in 1952; they rose to 30 percent in 1968; peaked at 36 percent in 1976; and generally remain about 30 percent (Niemi and Weisberg, 1984, 394).

Further change has been noted by students of electoral behavior. They have witnessed increased ticket splitting, in which voters either choose candidates of both parties for different offices or simply skip voting for some offices (Wattenberg, 1984, 17–23).

Along with changes in party identification and voting, there is still a reluctance to argue that a true realignment has occurred. This is true of academic analysts (e.g., Lipset, 1985), informed journalists (e.g. Schneider, 1984), or those engaged in polling for the apparently stronger Republican Party (e.g., Teeter, 1984). Many commentators are still urging us to wait for the next election. If they mean the election of 1988, when the Republicans will be without the immensely popular Ronald Reagan, then the same wait-and-see attitude can be predicted after that election as well.

Without directly entering the debate on the imminence of realignment, it is possible to outline four sets of circumstances that bear on its possibility. These involve changing circumstances, changes in the composition of the groups aligned with particular parties, changes in the political parties, and the mobilization of new groups.

Changing Circumstances

One example of the way voters and political parties are shaped by the settings in which they are found comes from the experiences of Western European socialist parties. Almost all share a characteristic weakness at this time, and one argument is that they are victims of their past success (Wolfe, 1985). That is, the policies of socialist parties to increase representation for working-class interests, improve working conditions, provide broad coverage of social welfare, and generally ease the impact of industrialism without seriously disrupting social and political traditions have, in fact, all paid off. Unwilling to move in an increasingly radical direction, and without new and attractive programs to offer, they have become weakened and have lost electoral support to more conservative parties (Przeworski, 1985).

On the other side of the political spectrum are the experiences of pre–World War II Germany. Military defeat and forced reparations, adjustment to new political boundaries and new forms of government, all in the context of serious economic dislocations that would eventually be worldwide, forced existing political parties to redefine their policy positions. The centrist parties became more conservative than they had been initially. While the Socialist and Communist parties saw no need for policy shifts, their appeal remained confined to the working class, and, as problems became more severe, the more extreme solutions offered by the Communists seemed more attractive. Finally, it was left to the newly emerging Nazi movement to pick themes from both left and right and turn them into an even more attractive message, rooted in the traditions of German nationalism (Hamilton, 1982; Abel, 1966).

The contrast between Catholics in Europe and the United States has always been a striking one, with the former more often aligned with conservative parties and the latter with the Democrats. The reasons for this difference are totally circumstantial and not of theological origin. This topic was discussed earlier when the sources of alignment stimulated by the experiences of newly arrived Catholics in the cities were described. In Europe, at least prior to World War II, communities were more stable and more effectively under the influence of the Church hierarchy. Most practicing Catholics were then kept from identifying with the anticlericalism of liberal parties or the antireligiosity of Socialist and Communist parties.

Conditions affecting the political alignment of Catholics and the unique aspects of their experiences in the United States are demonstrated by contrast with Canada. Liberalism and anticlericalism (and a desire for union with the United States) were represented in 19th-century Lower Canada (now Quebec) by the Rouges movement (Bernard, 1971). After Confederation in 1867 allowed the British North American colonies to unite into a single nation, the minority Rouges were absorbed into the opposition Liberal Party. At the same time, the Catholic clergy in Quebec were preaching their variant of French Canadian nationalism by supporting the dominant Liberal-Conservative Party, the precursor of the modern Conservative Party, and this was the political outlet for the Church faithful. Canada, in other words, displayed alignments similar to those of continental Europe. However, once the Liberal Party gained national office, the disadvantages of total support for the Conservatives by French Canada were soon apparent. As the so-called "Holy War" heated up in Quebec, Liberal supporters appealed to the pope, arguing that the Canadian Liberal Party was not at all like similarly named European ones. The clergy remained adamant in their opposition to the Liberals just as ordinary Quebec voters were drawn to them. Voters in French Canada were affected by distaste for the Conservative handling of the uprising led by folk hero Louis Riel and pride in the Liberal Party leadership of fellow Quebecker Wilfrid Laurier (Wade, 1968, 356–382). Once Laurier became the Liberal Party's Prime Minister, French Canadian laity were brought into the Liberal fold, and their voting attachments came to resemble those of coreligionists in the United States.

Changing Group Composition

The political difference between European and U.S. Catholics has now declined for two opposite reasons. The influence of the Church over its parishioners has abated in Europe, while U.S. Catholics have become more conservative. This conservatism has always been present, well described by Rossiter (1962). What changed is the growing coincidence between the conservative ideals of Catholics and their political behavior. This was already detected in Catholic voting behavior in the 1950s. The move back to the Democrats following the nomination of John F. Kennedy was not a return home after a temporary lapse but a momentary halt in a long-term trend. Catholic political loyalty, formed at an earlier time, might have continued in the same direction if new generations of Catholics had been bound by the same forces. But higher education, better paying jobs, and a more permissive society all contributed to loosening the bonds of Catholic communal existence. Perceived at this level, greater numbers of Catholics are now voting their pocketbooks.

Some of the continuity of social values and practices is ensured through the process of socialization. In the political world there is a comparable form of political socialization (Jennings and Niemi, 1981). Social mobility always presents some hurdle to passing on partisan attachments across generations, yet without ever totally blocking their continuity. On the face of it, generational political similarities have appeared stronger in Europe than in the United States. For example, in a study done in the 1950s, Almond and Verba (1963, 132–139) found that the greatest opposition to cross-party marriage partners or playmates for children was, in descending order, present in Italy, Mexico, Germany, Great Britain, and the United States. Opposition to social intercourse with opposition parties was rooted in the clearly understood ties between partisanship and social characteristics, especially religious observance, a tie that U.S. respondents were less likely to recognize. But since most marriage partners and playmates are chosen from among those with whom there is greatest social contact, and these are more likely to be people similar in class, ethnic, religious, and racial background, even in the United States there will be a tendency to have social contacts with the politically like-minded. At times there will even be overt acknowledgement of these tendencies, particularly in areas where the legacy of the Civil War is still meaningful. For example, historian Allen Howard of Southern Illinois University tells me that, in the southern Illinois community where he grew up, his generation, born just before World War II, was the first to intermarry. There, intermarriage meant marrying across party lines.

While generational continuity provides an important underpinning for political alignments, it is also the wedge allowing for changes in them. Significant events affecting a generation—for example, the Civil War, Great Depression, mass migration—have the potential for shaping its political outlook and behavior. As we get closer to the present, it is not always easy to think of comparable formative experiences that affect an entire generation. The youth revolution of the 1960s would appear to qualify as a worldwide phenomenon. In the United States, it primarily affected blacks who were responding to changes in civil rights and those of college-educated or more privileged backgrounds—often the two characteristics were combined (Matthews and Prothro, 1966, 407–440; Keniston, 1965; Flacks, 1971). It is largely from the more privileged that the new political independents emerged. Initially, when they participated, they were most likely to support the Democrats, but more recently they moved to the Republicans. At the same time, many of their social characteristics might lead one to expect that they were potentially Democrats.

Changing Parties

The fact that political parties are organizations gives them a continuity that extends beyond the results of particular elections. Similarly, continuity derives from the reasons parties give for their existence and from the programs and policies for which they stand. This is not to say that all parties remain the same for all times. As organizations, they are affected by their relative success, by the decisions they make, and the kinds of leaders they permit to emerge. Whiteley's examination of the British Labour Party (BLP) relates the decline in its support to "failures of policy performance" (Whiteley, 1983, 1). Whiteley looks for sources of failure in how the party operated, not in transformations of the society in which it is found. He is then able to draw attention to the effects, first, of the BLP's governing experience and, then, of its oppositional role, when it came under increased pressure from extraparliamentary party components that have a recognized place in party decision-making, in particular, from militant trade union leaders. The latter influenced its move to greater ideological consistency, leading to internal battles between the left and right wings of the party. The latter, representing the pragmatic, non-Marxist coalition of social reformers and traditional union leaders, broke away in 1981 to form the Social Democratic Party. As a result, the BLP is no longer the same party it was, say, in 1945.

Today we may be inclined to forget the significance of the Republican Party's association with abolition and the way in which this association established political loyalties for black voters. While these ties had begun to unravel in northern cities, as black voters came under the domination of urban political machines, their loyalty was not fully shaken until the presidential election of 1936. In other words, northern blacks—there was no significant black voting in the South at this time—were slower to experience the effect of the New Deal. Local conditions also inhibited change where, in Chicago for example, there was no significant black presence in the Democratic machine until 1939 (Gosnell, 1935; J. Wilson, 1960, 50).

Southern influence on the Democratic Party remained strong, and it was not until the presidency of Lyndon Johnson, himself a southerner, that the Democrats became associated with a major struggle for the extension of civil rights to blacks. Southern white voters were now presented with their normal party choice in a new form. Change in the policy position of the Democratic Party, then, was in itself an important stimulus to moving southern whites out of the Democratic Party and into the Republican fold (Sundquist, 1973, 245–274). Like the BLP today, the Democratic Party has undergone transformations in its character.

Mobilizing New Participants

A final source of change occurs when new groups are mobilized into the political system and, through their participation, alter the outcome of political contests. Andersen (1979) argues that it was this kind of "electoral replacement" involving new, formerly unaffiliated or nonparticipating groups that resulted in the realignment of the 1930s. It is an argument that is empirically easier to sustain than the contrary one, that changing alignments occur through the large-scale conversion of existing voters. Her thesis is consistent with the transformation of British politics and the virtual disappearance of the Liberal Party after World War I, when the British Labour Party acquired sufficient organizational strength and electoral credibility to gain support of working-class voters. If the latter had previously voted, they would have been most likely to select Liberal candidates, although their subsequent defection was not in itself enough to cause the disintegration of the Liberal Party.

Expectations that inclusion of other large groups will alter political alignments have not always proved true. For example, the enfranchisement of women did not appear to lead to any major changes in voting profiles in the United States or even in other countries. Historically, women's political participation has tended to be less than that of males, and it has only become equal as women have increasingly worked outside the home (Poole and Ziegler, 1985, 127–129). Even then, there did not appear to be much difference in the voting behavior of the sexes, except in some European countries, where women made more conservative choices. During the 1984 U.S. presidential election, there was considerable talk about the "gender gap" (Keeter, 1985, 101–104). The expectation was that large numbers of women would be more inclined to vote for the Democratic Party, in part because of their perceptions of President Reagan as more likely to lead the country into war (e.g., Frankovic, 1982, 439–448). The outcome of that election indicated that the gap was much smaller than anticipated, and, in any case, whatever difference in outlook may have existed between men and women was offset by other sources of political attachment (Pomper, 1985, 70; Keeter, 1985, 92).

Questions about the relative importance of the conversion of longtime voters versus the mobilization of new ones have been central to understanding the success of the Nazi Party. We know that there was a sharp increase in turnout between the elections of 1928 and 1933, the final free one until after World War II. One formerly prominent thesis was that those recruited into the Nazi movement, propelling it into its successful position, came mainly from the alienated, previously nonvoting public (Lipset, 1981, 148–152). In the most recent and thorough analysis of voting results, Hamilton (1982) tends to ignore this issue and concentrates instead on the class basis of voting for the Nazi Party. We can infer both from changes in turnout and from Hamilton's analysis that the weakness of the party structure in the Weimar Republic, augmented by the exclusion of the working class up until World War I, meant that many Germans did not have a firm attachment to any political party. The exceptions were those militant workers who were tied to socialist and communist movements and the relatively small numbers of the middle class with strong commitment to center and right-wing parties tied to prewar experiences. The rise of the Nazi movement then is not easily accounted for in terms of some wide-scale conversion simply because there was not much difficulty in breaking with the past. It was mobilization that was the most important source of realignment (Brown, 1987).

CLEAVAGES, ALIGNMENTS, AND EVERYDAY LIFE

Summary

By beginning this chapter with social cleavages, our perspective is widened to the total society. In the politics of everyday life, sources of social and political differentiation permeate virtually every aspect of existence. When alignments are introduced as a way of giving political direction to cleavages, a link is suggested between society and state. Alignments, then, reveal the extent to which cleavages have become translated into political attachments or actions.

Kinship was treated here as the fundamental basis of social organization, out of which grow identifications of race, ethnicity, language, and nationality. The primitive nature of these social bonds and the affective loyalties they generate make them of lasting importance. When they also become politicized, they can divide a society until it breaks apart in civil war or revolution. Even when such kinship-derived ties lie dormant, as they may do most of the time, they never lose their potency because they are related to the most frequent forms of interpersonal interaction. As long as people live in families and value the family's continuity, parochial and tribal loyalties have the potential for entering the political arena.

Cleavages that grow out of the division of labor are similarly universal and sustained by interpersonal relations, but they are less often political. Reasons for the lower likelihood that class will be politicized, apparently contrary to the thesis that "the history of all hitherto existing society is the history of class struggles" (Marx and Engels, 1959, 7), are discussed in the following chapter. While it is possible that reasons for national differences in class alignments can be found in the ways in which class is conceptualized and measured (a problem of sociological theory), our concerns will be with the avenues available for the expression of class interests (a problem of class mobilization and actions).

Attention to the political relevance of age and sex demonstrates how cleavages may alter their significance over time. Moreover, even though age and sex may not be associated with distinct alignments toward a single movement or party, they can still be important because of the way they lead to political action.

Though we present cleavages as stable social divisions, they are not immune to change. Political alignments start by being less stable than social divisions and they too change over time. Our concern with mobilization in Chapter 3 is premised on the importance of changing circumstances in predicting whether a social group is ready to take action politically. In the concluding examples from university life, we have a transition between the topics of this chapter and their expression in the next one.

Locating a University Campus

In February 1965 the Chicago Circle campus of the state University of Illinois opened as a four-year college in its newly built west-side location. Its placement in the city from which the existing university in downstate Urbana received the largest share of its students was part of a continuing effort to expand educational opportunities, initially for World War II veterans and then for those of working-class and minority backgrounds. This objective should be understood in the context of a system of higher education that was highly selective on the basis of class, religion, and race until the end of World War II (Levine, 1986, 136–161). Even the 1863 enabling legislation for land grant universities, which led to the founding of the University of Illinois in 1867, did not eliminate these distinctions, although it contributed to the stratification among universities. A major impetus to change came when the GI Bill of Rights gave World War II veterans the opportunity to use their benefits to complete schooling (K. Olson, 1974).

From 1945, when a still obscure state senator from Chicago, Richard J. Daley, first introduced a bill to locate a branch campus of the University of Illinois in Chicago, until 1963, when the U.S. Supreme Court rejected the final appeal by a community group opposed to the site selected, the issue dramatized conflicts between working class and middle class, black and white, men and women, technicians and politicians, city and suburb, Chicago and downstate. Individuals and groups representing the various interests played out their concerns within the legislature, the university, other public bodies, and the mass media. In addition, questions of where to locate the campus pitted university administrators against legislators, private against public universities, and publicly elected university trustees against other public officials (Banfield, 1961, 159–189; Rosen, 1980). Two illustrations from the process of locating a Chicago campus give concrete demonstrations of the continuous relevance of social cleavages and their ties to political actions.

Among early opponents of a campus in downtown Chicago were Illinois alumni: ''A few leading spirits among them were very much against anything that might give the University the reputation of being a 'poor boy's college' or, above all, a 'Negro's college' '' (Banfield, 1961, 160). The initial hurdles over location in the metropolitan region had been removed by 1957, when a bill for a Chicago campus was introduced in the General Assembly. Now disputes centered on whether the campus should be in the city or suburbs. One advocate of a Chicago site was a black Democrat from the city who took the position that the campus ''should not be a country club. . . . Students should be able to ride a streetcar to school; poor boys and girls couldn't afford automobiles'' (Banfield, 1961, 186). His views were contradicted by another black legislator from Chicago, a Republican,[1] who explained,

> The South Side Negro . . . doesn't go to college just to prepare for a job; going is part of the status pattern. The middle-class Negro is the one who goes to college, and he goes as an expression of his drive upward in the status pattern. Most Negroes who would go to the University probably have their own cars and would go regardless of location. (Banfield, 1961, 187)

After years of negotiation, selection of the present site was approved in 1961, only to arouse protest from area residents fearing displacement, though they were presumably to be served by the new campus. The locus of protest was in a group of women led by Florence Scala, who brought together members of the Italian community along with blacks, Mexicans, Puerto Ricans, and Greeks to join in picketing, sit-ins, and public meetings. ''They were embarrassing to the mayor, who knew how to deal with men but was uncomfortable in dealing with actively protesting women'' (Rosen, 1980, 118). Moreover, especially for women from the Italian community, these protest activities were totally out of keeping with gender expectations:

> Alderman Marzullo supported the mayor, in part because he objected to the unorthodox methods of protest used by the women, whom he considered ''a bunch of crazies.'' Many men living in the area worked for the city and owed their jobs to the local political organization; they were not willing to jeopardize these jobs by opposing the city. (Rosen, 1980, 119)

What was to have been the opening to new educational opportunities was bought at great cost, activating virtually every significant line of cleavage. The location of the new campus illustrates how cleavages relate to politics and how close to the surface are the conflicts they generate.

NOTE

1. In the multimember Illinois House, abolished after a 1980 referendum, three members were elected from each district under a system of cumulative voting. Because of informal agreement between the two parties, this system virtually guaranteed that the third seat would go to the minority party in each district. One manifestation was the election of Republicans in solidly Democratic Chicago.

CHAPTER 3

MOBILIZING FOR ACTION

INTRODUCTION

The connection between cleavage-based groups and political alignments is provided by mobilization. That is, social cleavages become politically relevant when they are the basis of political action. Individuals and groups can be said to be mobilized when they are ready to act.

Readiness to act, in turn, is dependent on two different sets of processes. On the one hand, it requires conditions that will transform a social aggregate into a self-conscious group. Marx and Engels were concerned only with the relevance of working-class consciousness, but the processes they described, setting in motion conditions for mobilization, can be generalized to many other groups.

On the other hand, mobilization requires opportunities for action—access to resources that enable a previously deprived group to alter its conditions. These resources are rarely easy to acquire, making it difficult for excluded groups to become fully mobilized.

For followers of Marx, expectations of mobilization imply that a mobilized working class will be directed into a movement for the radical restructuring of society. In this regard the United States seems like an anomaly, and many explanations have been offered for U.S. exceptionalism. At the same time it is possible to see, in the lack of socialism in the United States, the difficulties that generally deter working-class mobilization.

Political action of a sustained character requires a stable organizational structure. Although many have argued that, for this purpose, a bureaucratic structure is both necessary and inevitable, bureaucratization is not the only possible outcome. Not only are there viable alternatives in social movement organizations, but U.S. political parties also display long-lived organizational variants.

Evaluating mobilization requires making normative judgments about the value of citizen participation. By doing so, we can then understand why some see dangers in too much mobilization and others in too little. The contemporary situation of university students provides another perspective on the prospects and consequences of mobilization.

CONDITIONS OF MOBILIZATION

Working in Factories

When Karl Marx and Friedrich Engels were asked to write a manifesto for the upcoming Communist International by a group of expatriate German workers living in England, they ended in producing a capsule theory of how any people, sharing some characteristic, are transformed into a politically aware group. For Marx and Engels (1959, 7), the only relevant shared characteristic was derived from relations to the means of production. But their insights were such that they can be extended to other characteristics that are the basis of major social cleavages. To begin with, they pointed out the significance of shared experiences, specifically, being in positions where people do not own the means of production. Those shared conditions define the boundaries of what they called "a class in itself." More generally, Gamson (1968) has called such categories of people "potential partisans" in anticipation of the possibility that the experiences they have in common can be tapped to form a consciousness of shared fate. The emergence of such consciousness was, to Marx and Engels, a turning point, transforming a class in itself to a class for itself.

Marx and Engels attributed the rise of class consciousness to the development of capitalism, but it may be more precise to say that it is associated with the emergence of factories. So, in newly industrializing countries, Inkeles and Smith (1974) have demonstrated the importance of factory work for creating a "modern" outlook. What appears to have been crucial in economic enterprises prior to industrialization was the restricted nature of contacts among workers. With industrialization, instead of work going to workers, workers came to a factory where they would be subject to the discipline of machines. As large numbers of workers would assemble together day after day, taught to come to the factory on time, to work in an orderly fashion, and even to understand the rudiments of competitive pricing, Marx and Engels hoped that they would soon realize that their destiny lay in their special position. Workers could witness the generality of exploitation; they had the opportunity to communicate with each other; they had been provided with the means of organizing and even taught the significance of organizing. From these conditions Marx and Engels predicted there would arise a class consciousness.

If the factory is important because it provides a milieu within which large numbers of people experience similar conditions about which they are able to communicate with each other, we should be alert to other kinds of settings where similar social processes take place. Clearly, the university is just such a setting. The political activism of students in the late 1960s and early 1970s was associated with demographic changes, resulting in a sharp increase in the college-age population, and subsequent ecological changes, in which the probabilities of interaction increased through college attendance.

Religion and Nationalism

Prior to the industrial revolution in Europe, the rise of nationalism and the Protestant Reformation came together to effect mobilization along cleavages of religious, ethnic, and linguistic differences. When Martin Luther posted his theses on the Wittenberg church door in 1517, he was voicing a personal protest that would find support in many circles. If the Catholic Church had held its former dominance over all of Europe, Luther's challenge to it could have been met with punishment by the secular authorities. He survived and lived to lead a branch of the Protestant Reformation because his questioning of religious authority was also an opportunity to question secular authority (Scribner, 1986). The German princes who protected Luther from the Catholic Church were themselves searching for opportunities to break the secular power of the Holy Roman Empire. Luther provided religious justification for these nationalistic stirrings. The German princes could provide similar protection to those who lived in their states and were amenable to following Luther. By translating the Bible into German, Luther introduced a means of education and communication that could readily extend beyond a religious subject matter. Mobilization in this period came about not only through common experiences of life under Catholicism remote from the geopolitical center of the Catholic Church, but also directly from religious and political movements, mediated through rising literacy that used the Bible as its common link. The result was an initial identification as both Protestants and German nationals.

A somewhat similar story could be told slightly later in England. There the Tudor kings had accumulated independent wealth for the Crown, both giving them some independence from Parliament and enabling them to pay for the personal loyalty of household guards and troops. Experience of the Wars of the Roses (1455–1485) had taught the English nobility the importance of a stable central authority, even though they had no wish for that authority to become burdensome. In light of this, Henry VIII's desire for a male heir had a plausibility that could overcome qualms about the propriety of divorcing his queen. Henry may not have been deeply concerned with religion, but he needed the legitimacy that came from religious support (Smith, 1953, 208; Smith, 1971, 117–118). Nationalism and national interests again coincided with rising Protestantism to mobilize a changing ruling class, and through them, their supporters and dependents (Smith, 1953, 166).

The English and German examples of mobilization differ from Marx's analysis of the emergence of class consciousness in being restricted to narrower segments of the population yet eventually serving to mobilize much larger numbers than the factory workers about whom Marx was concerned. In all cases, however, shared conditions as a basis for recognizing an identity of interest are crucial. Those shared conditions are not in themselves sufficient to guarantee mobilization, and recent students of social movements have turned instead to "resource mobilization." That is, mobilization occurs when a previously disadvantaged group is able to gain access to and control over resources (McCarthy and Zald, 1973). Resources can be of many different kinds—time to go to meetings, the ability to speak in public, writing skill, knowing how to run a meeting, the ability to enlist supporters and allies, understanding when circumstances can be turned to advantage. Attention to resources helps explain why movements spread, as Wuthnow (1985, 811–813) argues in the case of the widespread adoption of Protestantism in 16th-century England, where resources fostering Protestantism belonged to the king and a supportive Parliament in opposition to the rural aristocracy.

Resources in themselves do not explain how the initial stimuli that led to organization came into being. That question can only be answered when resources are related to social cleavages, understood as criteria for allocating scarce resources. To the extent that these cleavages are the basis for differential allocation, then they have the potential for defining any form of inequality as politically relevant.

OPPORTUNITIES FOR MOBILIZATION

Access to Resources

The resource mobilization perspective argues that collectivities, no matter how aggrieved, will not be able to act together unless they acquire the necessary resources. It does not address the question of how these resources can be acquired. For that we need to look at the external environment in which potentially mobilizing individuals and groups are found. Within that environment will be found other groups, already mobilized, some of whom control important resources. For those not yet mobilized, the trick is to gain access to those resources.

There will be occasions when more privileged groups are willing to open pathways to mobilization. They may do so inadvertently, as they go about protecting their own resources. For example, Marx praised the bourgeoisie for saving the working class from "rural idiocy" by providing workers with their first political education. He described this process as occurring when factory owners instructed workers in the rudiments of economics to persuade them that they needed to help owners compete. It was from such a source, according to Marx, that workers recognized that they could use the same tools in their own interests (Marx and Engels, 1959, 15–16).

Dominant groups may be prepared to share the means for successful mobilization with a disadvantaged group even more overtly. Such interaction occurs when the dominant groups are looking for allies in a larger competitive arena. For example, in Wyoming and Utah women were given the right to vote in the latter part of the 19th century, prior to the successful conclusion of the struggle for national suffrage and without the help of organized women's groups. Grimes (1967) argues that women won the right to vote in frontier areas precisely because there were so few politically conscious women in a society that was otherwise unstable and unruly. Women were invited to participate in the expectation that they would be supportive of stable values and institutions.

In pre–World War I Britain, women, mainly from the middle and upper classes, had already begun to mobilize to gain suffrage. With other channels of political action limited, they engaged in acts of civil disobedience. When Britain entered the war in 1914, such acts of defiance became more threatening, and, in addition, as men were called for active duty, women could often take their place in the labor force. Many activist women were then placated with promises of suffrage rights after the war if they would support the war effort and refrain from civil disobedience. That promise was fulfilled through limited suffrage rights in 1918 (Rover, 1967).

When workers were agitating for political recognition and the full rights of citizenship in 19th-century Britain, there were some in the Conservative Party who agreed with future Prime Minister Benjamin Disraeli's assessment that the working class was really made up of "angels in marble" (a phrase from *The Times* obituary for Disraeli), who, given the right to participate, would be among the supporters of conservative policies and the Conservative Party (McKenzie and Silver, 1968). The subsequent passage of the Reform Bill of 1867 confirmed the Conservative Party's resilience as the party of government.

It is probably more usual for those who control resources to do everything they can to retain their control and for those able to participate to do what they can to keep the disadvantaged from mobilizing. So the rights of British workers to form trade unions and to vote did not occur through some peaceful evolution, where those in control decided it was time to extend citizen rights to workers. Rights were acquired only after decades of political agitation and acts of violence by relatively small numbers of workers, often linked by only the loosest organizational bonds. Whether or not we agree with Thompson (1966, 711–832) that there was a unified working-class consciousness early in English history, discussed in Chapter 4, it is still clear that the general mobilization of workers did not occur until they had the legal right to organize.

U.S. Blacks

The importance of legal barriers to mobilization is also illustrated by the experiences of blacks in the U.S. South. For a brief period after the Civil War, political participation, including electoral participation, was high (Perman, 1987, 67–70). Soon, however, whites moved to reassert their power. Violence and threats of violence served to discourage black participation, but because the use of such naked power is itself an expensive resource and raises the possibility of legal retaliation, white ruling groups moved to institute legal restrictions. Poll taxes, literacy tests, and grandfather clauses were introduced to insure the legal disfranchisement of blacks, as well as of many poor whites who had otherwise supported the Populists. In this way, dissent was repressed and the need for white unanimity was affirmed on the grounds that "people of an occupied land must bury their differences and join forces to repel the alien" (Key, 1949, 552). From then until civil rights finally became established in the South, southern blacks were limited in the settings and occasions when they could associate without arousing suspicion.

Because church was one of the few places where blacks could assemble freely, it was essential to the black civil rights movements as the latter got under way in the 1950s (Oberschall, 1973, 220–222). In church, blacks could acquire organizing skills and even compensate for the deficiencies of public education. It followed that black ministers could acquire the role of political leaders more readily than others could.

> Southerners are church-going people, and the church offers the only public gathering in which many Negro southerners find Negro points of view openly advocated.
>
> The Negro minister is highly visible, then, and his professional role requires him to serve as a spokesman within the Negro community. The forensic and organizational skills developed in that role also equip Negro ministers to serve as spokesmen to the white community. Moreover, because they are not directly dependent on whites for their income as most southern Negroes are, any propensity to serve as an interracial spokesman is not inhibited by economic constraints. Indeed, the fact that he is "of the cloth" may ensure the Negro minister a modicum of respect, however condescending, from local whites. (Matthews and Prothro, 1966, 180)

As the history of U.S. blacks illustrates, mobilization is a difficult process, requiring both awakening the consciousness of an incipient group and penetrating existing political structures. Some members of the group undergoing mobilization must be willing to put themselves on the line for their beliefs—sacrificing personal and familial comforts, working long hours with little guarantee of success, perhaps threatened by imprisonment or even death. Meanwhile, if their targets are existing political organizations and their representatives, they frequently find the latter insulated from importuning outsiders and resistant to change.

WHY NO SOCIALISM IN THE UNITED STATES?

Is the United States an Anomaly?

By starting the discussion of mobilization in this chapter with Marx, we have emphasized two themes: the importance of shared conditions and the need for stimulation of group consciousness. Also implied, however, is the direction of actions that will be taken by a mobilized group. For Marx, class consciousness, by which he meant working-class consciousness, could only lead to revolution and the eventual creation of the dictatorship of the proletariat. The road to that goal would be achieved by socialist and communist movements. In other words, anything other than a separate political association aimed at achieving working-class goals was either a manifestation of "false consciousness" or a deluded hope that those goals could be reached by cooperating with other classes. The problems raised by this perspective in evaluating the nature of working-class mobilization are especially well-illustrated by the situation of the United States.

To observers of mass industrialization, the United States seemed the perfect setting for the mobilization of workers into a political movement; the only question was when it would occur. Writing to Joseph Weydemeyer in 1852, Marx judged the United States to still be too "underdeveloped" to give rise to the kind of class struggle that would herald a proletarian revolution (Marx and Engels, 1959, 456–457). Forty years later, Engels would complain that the German socialists who had emigrated to the United States were not able to create a major socialist workers' party, in part because of their own shortcomings. But he recognized that even more important were the conditions present in the United States: the electoral system of "winner take all"; the divisions among workers according to birthplace, ethnicity, and race; and the relative prosperity of workers (Marx and Engels, 1959, 457–458). Additional reasons were suggested by Turner's (1947) 1893 paper "The Significance of the Frontier in American History," either by using the expansion of western settlement as the key to explaining the absence of class distinctions or, when used by Marxists, to account for the absence of class consciousness (Sweezy, 1972, 147–165).

At least since the early part of the 19th century, workers in the United States have organized into their own political movements and into trade unions. With the New Deal, organized labor became an active part of the Democratic Party (Greenstone, 1969, 39–80). Up to the present, the majority of its members have supported Democratic candidates for office. Most recently, even the popularity of President Reagan did not overwhelmingly attract union households (which include more than union members)—48 percent indicated a vote for President Jimmy Carter and another 6 percent for John Anderson in 1980, and 53 percent voted for Walter Mondale in 1984 (New York Times/CBS poll in Pomper, 1985, 67).

Still the question, first posed in this form by Sombart (1976) in 1906, of "why no socialism?" remains. Answers offered cover the whole range of social, political, economic and cultural factors that characterize life in the United States, repeating themes from Marx, Engels, and Turner and adding others, like the absence of feudalism (Hartz, 1955). (For a thorough summary, see Lipset, 1977, 31–149.) In effect, these answers tend to be dismissive of past and existing workers' movements. At the same time, they see the political relevance of trade unions as compromised by their incorporation into the existing party system. It is as though there were no authentic working-class mobilization.

Barriers to Working-Class Mobilization

It is possible to see the apparent exceptionalism of U.S. class politics as only a matter of degree. For example, while Lipset (1968) studied socialism in Canada as a way of understanding the lack of a viable socialist party in the United States, anyone who looks primarily at Canada finds that socialism there is limited in its own way (Penner, 1977). Canadian voting studies provide evidence that class is a relatively weak political cleavage (Clarke et al., 1979). Similarly, while Britain has both greater class consciousness and a working-class party, it still appears defective to those who compare Britain to continental Europe. The British Labour Party was never totally the political arm of a unified working class, and approximately half the electorate of working-class background vote for the Conservative Party (Butler and Stokes, 1969; Rose, 1980, 156–161). Marx's theoretical standards for mobilization do not merit blind acceptance if only because the historical conditions of industrialization simply vary too greatly from country to country (e.g., Gallie, 1983).

Equating the lack of socialism with defective worker mobilization is ideologically grounded, to be sure, but, as a perspective, it is revealing of the general dilemmas associated with mobilization. We can agree that enfranchisement is a critical step in political mobilization where there are competitive elections, but beyond that point, it is not clear just what is created by the subsequent participation. Przeworski describes the dilemma of early socialist parties in mobilizing workers: "Political democracy, specifically suffrage, was a ready-made weapon for the working class. Was this weapon to be discarded or was it to be wielded on the road from 'political to social emancipation'?" (Przeworski, 1985, 8). Among the problems they faced was the need to develop as political instruments that could unify workers who otherwise compete with each other as much as they cooperate. Yet in the quest for electoral power, socialist parties will require allies from outside the working class to compensate for the minority status of workers. Enlisting such broad support will, in turn, dilute ideological purity. But failure to broaden the social base would doom socialist parties to ineffective minority status (Przeworski, 1985, 7–46), as the experiences of other groups demonstrate. For example, the women's movement tried to make a political impact through supporting a Women's Party, without any measure of success; in 1984 Jesse Jackson tried to create a "rainbow coalition" to reshape the Democratic Party in a way more responsive to special interests, but again without much success.

But the dilemmas do not end here. Groups lacking their own organizational outlet have little alternative for producing an impact on the political system. For example, a survey of political participation in the United States in the 1960s, in which participation was defined as acts directed to influencing government, found voting in presidential elections the most frequently reported act, while the incidence of more time-consuming and difficult activities dropped dramatically. Moreover, in almost all instances, participation was greatest among those of highest socioeconomic status (Verba and Nie, 1972). But if voting in presidential elections is the most frequent form of participation, where does that leave groups whose interests do not appear to be directly served by existing political parties? One answer emerges when the United States is compared to other countries with working-class parties. Lower rates of participation by those in lower socioeconomic status is partly a function of the absence of a working-class party in the United States, an absence that has never been adequately compensated by the Democratic Party (Lipset, 1981, 194–195). Still, surveys conducted in the mid-1970s in the United States, Britain, Germany, the Netherlands, and Austria that took into account both conventional and unconventional forms of political participation found that class differences, especially related to level of education, remained in all countries (Barnes and Kaase, et al., 1979).

THE IMPORTANCE OF ORGANIZATION

Organizational Muscle

Mobilization is a necessary step in preparation for action; action itself requires that a mobilized group be organized. An organization provides continuity by having an ongoing structure with which to respond to the stimuli of either internal or external problems. An organization exists as a communication network, enabling members, perhaps otherwise passive, to be called to action. This ability is one of the strengths of voluntary associations, like the American Medical Association, which are able to quickly mount lobbying and letter-writing campaigns (Yale Law Journal, 1954, 954–969). That capacity to inform members, mobilize newcomers, and enlist sympathetic supporters is part of the power of an organization. When an organization's representatives attempt to exert power over outsiders, they can do so to the extent that they have muscle behind their rhetoric, demonstrated most effectively by a mobilized following.

While we know from the organizational literature that there is no best form of organization (Scott, 1987), this now conventional wisdom has yet to be commonly accepted in considering political organization. Up until now the range of alternatives considered feasible have been restricted to two forms: bureaucracy or social movement, with preference for the former a long-standing tradition. Speaking of democratic working-class parties, and the German Socialists in particular, Michels saw no alternative to an organizational form that would allow combat readiness— "A fighting party needs a hierarchical structure" (Michels, 1962, 79). Yet this same kind of organization would lead inevitably to compromise of democratic ideals and practices through the establishment of an "iron law of oligarchy" (Michels, 1962, 342–356). If Michels and others after him would deplore these oligarchic tendencies, Lenin viewed them as positive forces:

> Members of the hostile parties in parliament often tease the Socialists by exclaiming: "Fine democrats you are indeed! Your movement is a working-class movement only in name; as a matter of fact it is the same clique of leaders that is always in evidence. . . ." The political ideas of the Germans have already developed sufficiently, and they have acquired enough political experience to enable them to understand that without the "dozen" of tried and talented leaders . . . professionally trained, schooled by long experience and working in perfect harmony, no class in modern society is capable of conducting a determined struggle. (Lenin, 1943, 113–114)

Organizational Forms

Working-class parties originating outside a parliamentary context have often attempted to attain political power by building their natural constituency into a cohesive, mass-based organization in ways appreciated both by Michels and Lenin, although not necessarily in the overtly undemocratic way the first deplored and the second welcomed. They have tried to achieve combat readiness and counteract the force of middle-class dominance pervading the society through schools, church, newspapers, and similar institutions by creating their own subsocieties. In these, party membership has extended to the provision of recreational activities, news sources, holiday camps, and consumer cooperatives. As a result, party organization has meant a full-time operation involving both paid staff and volunteers. The extreme form of such organization is all-inclusive, totalitarian parties like the Communist, Nazi, or other fascist parties (Neumann, 1956, 400–405).

Parties that originated from within parliament, in contrast, began with a loose organization tied to legislative activities and preparation for elections. With the extension of universal suffrage, a more permanent organization was needed, generally run by a small number of professional employees subordinate to the parliamentary party. To the extent that there are party members, they are a small proportion of the electoral support normally won (Duverger, 1963; Epstein, 1980). Yet even these distinctions have not remained fixed, as working-class parties have lost much of their inclusive character, and middle-class parties, like the British Conservative Party after its defeat by Labour at the end of World War II, moved to adopt a modest form of mass membership (McKenzie, 1964).

Because new political parties often have their basis in social movements and may begin by adopting unconventional forms of political action, particularly civil disobedience, their organizational character has not always been taken seriously. By coming from a theoretical approach prevalent in the United States prior to the 1960s, participation in social movements was seen as a rare phenomenon, based on relatively transitory feelings of discontent by people with only the loosest ties to each other. Such people, it was assumed, could be easily persuaded to engage in violent and even irrational acts (for a critique see Jenkins, 1983). Not only is there now much less emphasis on the nonrational aspects of social movements, but there is also greater recognition of their organized character (Zald and Asch, 1966). Within that more organized character, however, there may be an absence of most characteristics we associate with bureaucracy—hierarchy of authority, technical competence, separation of job from other roles, payment in money, impersonality.

A hierarchy of authority is the defining characteristic of bureaucracy; it may or may not be present in a social movement. A social movement offers the unique setting for the appearance of charismatic leadership like that given by Fidel Castro. But it may also rely on rational-legal authority, illustrated by Freeman (1975) in what she characterizes as the "older branch" of the women's movement. Since it grew out of existing organizations of business and professional women, it followed the associational structure familiar to them, manifested in the local, state, and national divisions of the National Organization for Women (NOW). Some movement adherents, however, may wish to avoid hierarchy at all costs. This approach was typical of Freeman's "younger branch" of the women's movement, which had its origin in the radical movement of the 1960s, where women often found themselves relegated to secondary roles. As a result, the major thrust of those in the younger branch was to concentrate on women themselves in order to change their environments. That is, the main concern was to raise the consciousness of women as a disadvantaged group and, in this way, bring about changes at the interpersonal level that would have consequences for the larger society. The organizational format most appropriate to this goal was found in small discussion groups without permanent leadership. These groups would subdivide once they reached a size that appeared to hinder equal participation.

Small size and equality of participation and responsibility are generally characteristic of political "cells," a form of organization especially fitting for illegal and clandestine groups whose survival would otherwise be jeopardized by the arrest of leaders or those with knowledge of the identity of other members (Duverger, 1963, 27–36, 37–40, 49–50).

The efficiency of a bureaucracy is dependent on hiring and promoting personnel with technical qualifications. In a voluntary association, such qualifications would only apply to full-time paid staff, not as a usual criterion for membership. For the most part, membership requires the paying of dues. Other kinds of involvement are anticipated to come from only a minority of the members, and even they may be called on at infrequent intervals. In political movements, however, expectations of member participation are high, to the extent of total commitment to their goals. Freeman describes how women in the younger branch experienced conflict between family, job, or school responsibilities and those to the movement, leading some to cut themselves off from contacts with everyone except other, equally committed women (e.g., Freeman, 1975, 115–116, 134–142). For them, the criterion of membership is wholehearted belief in the movement's ideals and wholehearted devotion to its work. Like other social movements totally dependent on the involvement of members, there is little room for the "free rider" who benefits from collective action but, because he or she expects others in similar situations to participate, simply enjoys the advantages of that participation without cost (Olson, 1971).

U.S. Parties

Whether a bureaucracy or a movement-like political organization is the more effective arm of a mobilized group, U.S. political parties may appear, at first sight, to be defective. This impression is conveyed in at least three ways: the absence of clearly identifiable party leaders, the decline of urban political machines, and the decline in voter turnout. The organization of U.S. political parties is such that "more than in any other type of formal organization, the official lines of authority are suspect, and there is always implicit the question, Who is the 'real' leader"

(Schlesinger, 1965, 177). These ambiguities are present both within and across local, state, and national levels (Sorauf and Beck, 1988, 73–100, 131–153). The problem lies not in the absence of authoritative actors but in the presence of a wide range of party actors who have access to many sources of power for dealing with the uncertainties of the electoral environment (Schwartz, 1990). In other words, consequential decisions can be made from a variety of loci, making a single hierarchy of authority impossible and authority itself unable to monopolize power. This may make U.S. political parties somewhat peculiar as organizations without negating their organizational character.

Up to the 1960s, local party organization displayed a variety of forms, the most elaborate of which is designated by Mayhew (1986, 19–20) as "traditional." Such organizations are autonomous, long-lasting, hierarchical, concerned with nominations for a variety of offices, and supported by workers who were, in some way, paid for their efforts. For Mayhew, the designation of organization as traditional stems from customary ways of viewing U.S. parties:

> The main tradition of work on American party structure has centered . . . on the country's elaborate system of local, state, and national patronage organization that took shape and gave politics and government a distinctive character in the nineteenth century and then settled into a long irregular decline during the twentieth. (Mayhew, 1986, 3)

But they are also traditional in Weber's (1978, I, 228) sense of the administrative structure associated with traditional bases of authority, where officials are bound to their patrons by personal ties of loyalty. Similar kinds of loyalty are required of party workers, notably in urban political machines (Gosnell, 1968; Guterbock, 1980), even when they are paid in money.

Changing conditions of government led to the decline of traditional party organizations, as have more recent pressures from rationalizing electoral activities. The apparent takeover of party functions by political action committees and the mass media has affected the Democratic Party most seriously.

> All three Democratic organizational bases of the 1960s (traditional party organizations, liberal activist groups, and labor unions) have deteriorated—unions have declined in membership, mobilizing power in elections, and influence in Congress as evidenced under Carter—and the party's procedures for nominating presidential candidates have not worked well since the 1960s. (Mayhew, 1986, 331)

But meanwhile, at both state and national level, the Republican Party has actually increased its organizational structure and coherence, and the Democrats have, to a degree, tried to catch up (Cotter et al., 1984). Distinctions then need to be made between parties and among levels, extending as well to an evaluation of their mobilizing powers. So, reviewing Burnham's (1983) volume on the crisis associated with low levels of electoral participation, Beatty recognizes the extent to which it characterizes different population groups and concludes: "Republicans are the single most mobilized group in our polity; they go to the polls as if they were banks, as indeed they are—for them'' (Beatty, 1983, 37). We should conclude from all of this that U.S. parties are not defective; they are simply "in the American mold" (Epstein, 1986).

EFFECTS OF MOBILIZATION

Too Much Mobilization?

Judging the effects of mobilization means interpreting past experiences or constructing probable outcomes in relation to some model of society. To the extent that models are conceptions of the ideal, they are also normative presumptions about the desirability of levels and kinds of participation by cleavage-based groups.

One set of assessments is tied to a concept of mass society that was most prevalent in Germany between the two world wars and associated with the work of Georg Simmel (1950). In this perspective, which once had a great deal of currency in sociology, modern society—industrial, urban, capitalist—was characterized by large numbers of rootless individuals whose experiences had left them detached from meaningful solidary structures like those that could grow out of religion or community. Because they were not protected by secondary structures, such individuals could be readily mobilized by elites, particularly of an exploitative, demagogic character (Kornhauser, 1959).

As a manifestation of this underlying perspective, some were led to argue that too much participation was a bad thing. For example, after studying voting behavior in a single community prior to the 1948 presidential election, where it was found that those least likely to vote were also those with the lowest level of interest in politics, the lowest level of education, and a low stake in community outcomes, it was concluded that it would be disadvantageous, if not even dangerous, to find means of encouraging the participation of such unpolitical types (Berelson, Lazarsfeld, and McPhee, 1954, 305–323). A similar argument has been a major theme in discussions of the rise of the Nazis, where the assumption had been that those who would normally not participate because they were alienated from normal political processes could be brought into the political arena only by way of extremist movements (e.g., Lipset, 1981, 148–152). A quite different set of concerns about excessive mobilization is present in Olson (1982). In evaluating the cost of mobilizing various interests, Olson considers the outcome to be eventually paralyzing to the political system because it cannot possibly meet all the demands placed upon it.

The Value of Mobilization

On the other side of the political spectrum are those unconvinced by arguments tied to the dangers of mass society. For example, Rogin (1967), looking at the kind of opposition aroused by the tactics of Senator Joe McCarthy's attack on apparent domestic subversion, dismisses the dangerousness of the masses as a specious argument. Instead, he sees it raised as a typically elitist fear of those perceived as a threatening underclass. In effect, he is buying into the more usual argument about the value of democratic participation—the more participation there is, the more responsive governing organs will be and the better the life of the society will be.

Rogin's perspective has a parallel to those who see mobilization, manifested in new social movements, as a vehicle of change. Without these movements, individuals would remain unconnected, interests unrepresented, and needs unmet (Oberschall, 1973; Gamson, 1968). Lipset (1977, 128), in reviewing the frequency and range of social movements in the United States, argues that they bring into the political system either a new or renewed concern with value premises that underlie political decisions. Initially, these are disruptive, but the fact that they deal with important values means that, eventually, they will become incorporated into existing political parties, thereby insuring that the latter alter their actions in ways that are responsive to changing conditions.

There will always be some skeptics who question whether mobilization produces policy changes, but the most careful scrutiny supports at least some relation. For example, Burstein's study of civil rights legislation led him to conclude that

> the weight of the evidence indicates that civil rights legislation in general, and EEO legislation in particular, passed as the result of long-term social changes manifested in public opinion and forced upon everyone's attention by the civil rights movement. (Burstein, 1985, 92)

The violence of that era was not directly productive of change, Burstein believes, but he feels it sensitized both the public and decision-makers to underlying problems. Similarly, Piven and Cloward (1971) argue that, under conditions of economic dislocation and collective violence, mobilization will lead public authorities to institute compensatory welfare policies, but they also see such policies, presented as signs of responsiveness but often only palliative measures, as the means elites can use to reestablish political control.

Mobilization is difficult for an excluded group and costly for the individual; yet, without mobilization, the group is powerless. One hundred fifty years ago, Tocqueville perceived the mobilization of U.S. citizens to be sustaining of democracy, counteracting tendencies to selfishness. Because of citizens' involvement in associations, Tocqueville felt, a state of mind was set in motion in which all problems were seen as solvable through collective action (Tocqueville, 1945, II, 114–118, 123–128). More recent observers, however, have been disturbed by evidence that most people know little about political issues, have little interest in politics, and do not seem to care who wins election. From such evidence, Neuman concludes that

> apathy dominates American mass politics. This has probably been true since the time of Alexis de Tocqueville, although in his time, as in ours, one is likely to get a contrary

impression as a result of the tiny minority of politically active and outspoken individuals who receive all the attention. (Neuman, 1986, 9)

Was Tocqueville then mistaken? Or is Neuman? We know that the world Tocqueville observed was very different from the present one. The United States was smaller and more homogeneous, its civic and political life primarily local, and its world status minor. Knowledge required for making intelligent decisions was readily accessible. Even if only minorities were politically aware and involved, they were probably representative of the major interests in the society. Not one of these conditions holds true today. At the same time, the rationale for mobilization remains unaltered. Without it, interests would remain unprotected and changes unchanneled.

Discontented Students

By now we should have a better understanding of the situation of the angry student, introduced in Chapter 1, as well as the reasons that other students could so easily empathize with her. The university controls valuable resources, organized in a bureaucratic structure within which almost all relationships of power put students at a disadvantage. The existence of widespread power differentials makes students a likely reservoir of discontent. But, as recent writing in social movements makes clear, discontent alone is not sufficient to bring about mobilization.

At the same time, the university provides an ideal situation in which mobilization can take place—participants come together for extended periods and they face similar conditions and problems. The political activities of college students during the late 1960s and early 1970s arose out of just such social settings. If mobilization leading to student action occurred in the recent past, why does it not occur today? The answers appear to lie both in the character of students at the University of Illinois at Chicago and in the environment they face.

The University of Illinois at Chicago is located near the downtown of a large metropolis. Except for the side of the campus on which all the health-related professional schools are located, there were no dormitories until the 1988–89 academic year. Commuting students, even if they no longer lived with their parents, were still not part of a resident university community. Further distraction was likely to arise from the fact that the large majority of students hold some off-campus employment. We can surmise from these characteristics that the typical UIC student is concerned with many important nonuniversity issues that would interfere with his or her direct mobilization. But even at UIC's sister campus in Champaign-Urbana, where there is a resident university community, there is currently an absence of student-based political activities on any appreciable scale. Because the status of student is a temporary one, life at the university can be treated as filled with discomforts that will pass, making it difficult to provide impetus to mobilization.

That observation leads to the further conclusion that the circumstances of prior mobilization were extraordinary. An unpopular war in Southeast Asia had a direct impact on students through the draft. It came at a time of major cultural changes stimulated by social movements of blacks and young people. The natural advantage of universities as settings for rapid communication among like-minded people was then enhanced by issues that were at the forefront of the political environment. It enabled students to call on allies outside the university and hence to expand their resources in ways that were an essential stage in the growth of the black civil rights movement, as Oberschall (1973, 217–218) points out. Unrest had an impact on university administrations. At UIC, for example, students were given representation in what had been a totally faculty senate, a student trustee was elected by his or her peers to serve as a nonvoting member of the University of Illinois Board of Trustees, and participation was encouraged in students' own governing association.

From the perspective of changing conditions on the campus, however, results have not been impressive. To be effective, there would need to be a greater investment of time than virtually any student can afford and a willingness for students and faculty to cooperate in advocating changes in the administrative structure that affects their day-to-day existence. Until those actions are forthcoming, students will endure their discomforts and complain as unconnected individuals.

CHAPTER 4
EXPLAINING
THE POLITICAL
WORLD

INTRODUCTION

Communication makes possible an awareness of group interests, allowing new groups to be mobilized and leading to the possibility of collective action. Up to now we have left unexplored the content of what is communicated or by what means it takes place. To treat these topics we need first to set aside sociological ambivalence about the role of ideas in human history and accept their capacity to be a moving force.

Coherent explanations of politics, organized into ideologies that have had major historical impact, include liberalism, conservatism, socialism, communism, and fascism. Each has national variations, and each is associated with the mobilization of social cleavages. While I treat the struggles for the rights of women and of ethnic and racial minorities as outgrowths of liberalism, it is also important to look at nationalism and feminism independently.

Attention to some of these ideologies in the United States confirms the way they acquire meanings specific to their national setting. In addition, they often appear to have limited relevance in explaining the political views of the ordinary citizen. It is not that such a person lacks the means to account for political events but rather that the explanations used are generally not rooted in historically significant ideological concepts. In distinguishing between the ideologies of intellectuals and political leaders, on the one hand, and the systems of meaning adopted by the general public, on the other, each should be given its appropriate weight.

Some form of ideology, whose message can be spread through a literate population, is essential for revolutionary social movements. In the United States, literacy has not been given much attention in comparison to the effects of the mass media in changing voters' minds. Rather than looking for specific changes, we should pay greater attention to other consequences of the mass media, especially their ability to spread political messages on a vast and rapid scale. Nor should we forget that the mass media have not totally superseded other means of communication for spreading political messages.

The chapter concludes by assessing the impact of ideology. Just as it is difficult to overcome structural barriers to mobilization, so it is difficult to discover the political ideas that will spark people to action.

SOCIOLOGICAL AMBIVALENCE

Do Ideas Count?

Most sociologists place a high value on being scientific. In the scientific world, explanations of past findings and expectations about future ones make up what are known as scientific theories. In the political world, such explanations and expectations are often called ideology. A political ideology may be regarded as a set of more or less coherent and durable ideas and beliefs that can be drawn upon for understanding and explaining political events. An ideology often contains a blueprint for the future, in the sense that it spells out the goals of a political movement or system. For some sociologists, this prescriptive content may be associated with pejorative connotations, as may the fact that the explanations offered are not subject to proof. Geertz (1973, 194) gives these objections a familiar construction—"I have a social philosophy; you have political opinions; he has an ideology."

Even more fundamental to sociologists' ambivalence about ideology is uncertainty about the role that ideas play in human history. That ambivalence is nowhere better illustrated than in the life and work of Karl Marx. An object of easily aroused ridicule for him was the "talker," the individual with schemes for remedying the ills of the world who had no true understanding of the course of history. Marx instead emphasized praxis, the plan of action leading to revolution (Avineri, 1968, 134–149). Or, as he put it in his criticism of the philosopher Feuerbach, "The philosophers have only *interpreted* the world, in various ways; the point, however, is to *change* it" (Marx and Engels, 1959, 245).

Marx conceived of ideology as epiphenomenal, that is, as growing out of economic experiences rather than having an independent character. Moreover, any ideology that did not have its roots in the experiences of an oppressed working class was, by definition, "false consciousness." Class consciousness, instead, was a form of collective self-awareness essential to revolutionary mobilization. At the same time, he recognized a role for intellectuals who would acknowledge the historical destiny of the working class and cast their lot with it. "Those bourgeois ideologists, who have raised themselves to the level of comprehending theoretically the historical movement as a whole" (Marx and Engels, 1959, 17) could play the role that I described in Chapter 3, referring to Marx and Engels' creation of a written workers' manifesto.

Ideology and Meaning

Among the founders of sociology, Max Weber stands out for his emphasis on the role of beliefs and values in affecting behavior. *The Protestant Ethic and the Spirit of Capitalism* (1958)—first published in 1904–05—is an exposition of how religious ideas affect religious behavior and, through them, other aspects of the life of the believer. The original beliefs can also become detached from their religious base and, in secularized form, continue to affect behavior generally, especially in the economic realm. In contrast, most of the sociology-of-knowledge tradition, whether stemming from Durkheim, Marx, or Mannheim, has treated ideas as derivative from their social origin and lacking the independent force necessary for affecting the course of history (Merton, 1957, 458).

Recent students of social movements, like Oberschall (1973), have tended to downplay the significance of ideology by seeing it as an important but hardly necessary component of movement existence or success. Such a judgment is based on an overly narrow concept of ideology, one that neglects the way social action is grounded in shared beliefs.

> The first step towards an understanding of a social movement suggests itself by common sense: we want to know what it is all about. . . . we want to know the entire complex of ideas, theories, doctrines, values, and strategic and tactical principles that is characteristic of the movement. We call this complex the *ideology* of the movement. (Heberle, 1951, 23–24)

In the sense intended by Heberle and used here, ideology is not confined to social movements, since similar understandings are part of all enduring social groups. This thought is expressed by Geertz in his definition of culture as "the structure of meaning through which men give shape to their experiences" and tied to politics as "one of the principal arenas in which such structures publicly unfold" (Geertz, 1973, 312).

But we must not place too heavy a burden on the concept of ideology itself. It is necessary to distinguish all-inclusive "grand" ideologies with elaborate and clearly defined substantive content, often associated with social movements, from segmented systems of meaning that may not have any overtly expressed and documented content. I begin with a selection of grand ideologies, those that are linked with major social cleavages, discussed in Chapter 2, and with their mobilization, discussed in Chapter 3.

IDEOLOGICAL CONCEPTS IN HISTORICAL CONTEXT

Liberalism

Searching for the oldest grand ideology of the modern world, we find liberalism, the ideology of modernism. If that selection comes as a surprise to those who anticipated that the oldest ideology would be a conservative defense of tradition, we should understand that tradition itself needs no defense unless it has been challenged. From his observation of non-Western traditional societies in this century, Geertz concludes that it is

> precisely at the point at which a political system begins to free itself from the immediate governance of received tradition, from the direct and detailed guidance of religious or philosophical canons on the one hand and from the unreflective precepts of conventional morality on the other, that formal ideologies tend first to emerge and take hold. (Geertz, 1973, 219)

Liberalism is not a single body of thought that emerged full-blown at one time or in one country. In England, liberalism had its origin in the political ascendancy of the Whigs—a combination of some elements of the old ruling class with religious dissenters and new men of wealth—following the Glorious Revolution of 1688 and its exposition in John Locke's (1966) *The Second Treatise of Government,* originally published in 1690. Later, John Stuart Mill, particularly in his 1848 work *Principles of Political Economy* (1965), would modify the original free market perspective with collectivist concerns for governmental protection (Hobhouse, 1911). On the European continent, liberalism went along with the Enlightenment. In France, for example, reaction to an absolute monarchy and a highly centralized Catholic Church stimulated both republicanism and anticlericalism. The ultimate assault on that traditional world came with the French Revolution, which was as much an ideology as a series of political events and, according to Tocqueville, was comparable to a religious revolution: "Not only did it have repercussions far beyond French territory, but like all great religious movements it resorted to propaganda and broadcast a gospel" (Tocqueville, 1955, 11).

Yet, despite its varied historical origins, it is still possible to see liberalism as a distinctive political orientation. Gray describes it as

> *individualist,* in that it asserts the moral primacy of the person against the claims of any social collectivity; *egalitarian,* inasmuch as it confers on all men the same moral status and denies the relevance to legal or political order of differences in moral worth among human beings; *universalist,* affirming the moral unity of the human species and according a secondary importance to specific historic associations and cultural forms; and *meliorist* in its affirmation of the corrigibility and improvability of all social institutions and political arrangements. (Gray, 1986, x)

Today, liberalism appears in two distinct guises—the classical laissez-faire view emphasizing the importance of individual freedom, including the right to private property; and the statist one, in which government assumes a protective role to buffer individuals from vagaries of the market.

By emphasizing the ways in which liberalism is the ideology of the modern world, one can discern its formative influences on such social movements and their related ideologies as the abolition of slavery, the struggle for women's rights, and the search for full rights of citizenship for excluded minorities (Marshall, 1964, 71–134).

Conservatism

Conservatism as a grand ideology had its beginnings in reaction to the French Revolution, modified, like liberalism, by national variations. Its dominant theme is protection of existing or traditional institutions and privileges. In the English-speaking world, the principal philosopher of conservatism is Edmund Burke, epitomized by the publication in 1790 of *Reflections on the Revolution in France* (1968). To Nisbet (1986), Burke is not simply one exponent of conservatism but its "prophet": "Rarely in the history of thought has a body of ideas been as closely dependent upon a single man and a single event as modern conservatism is upon Edmund Burke and his fiery reaction to the French Revolution" (Nisbet, 1986, 1). Burke combined support for God and king with an essentially pessimistic view of human nature and a belief in the limited capacity of human beings to respond to change. Specifically, the role he assigned to government was to control evil impulses that might otherwise run rampant.

Socialism

The Industrial Revolution created a new class of free workers, thrust into unprecedented and unsettling conditions (Kuczynski, 1967, 40–77), which provided the stimulus to fashioning an ideology that accepted the change from feudalism without accepting capitalism, at least not fully. The basis of a working-class ideology argued for more equitable redistribution of control over production and its rewards. While democratic socialism and totalitarian communism are worlds apart politically, they share a common philosophical heritage with respect to this view of the economic order, thereby justifying my shorthand approach here in speaking only of socialism.

Like both liberalism and conservatism, socialism too has its national variants, but its central focus has derived from the work of Karl Marx. Nothing approaches the influence of the *Manifesto of the Communist Party* for the whole range of people historically identified as Marxist socialists. Only in Britain and its former colonies has Marxism, as the dominant emphasis in the ideology representing working-class interests, been overridden by the strength of independent trade unionism and the intellectual influence of Fabians like Sidney and Beatrice Webb, who saw socialism evolving through reforms (Cole, 1937).

The summary picture of socialism given above has come to be characterized as the "old left." It is old in the sense that it is an ideology constructed on the basis of the dominance of productive forces at a time when the world economy is directed to consumption and provision of services. Out of this changed milieu, dissidents have constructed a "new left," premised on issues like "a clean environment, a better culture, equal status for women and minorities, the quality of education, international relations, greater democratization, and more permissive morality, particularly as affecting familial and sexual issues" (Lipset, 1981, 509–510). The new left has been caught up in lifestyle and social issues, the old left by economic ones, with inevitable conflict between the two (Lipset, 1981, 512–520; Howard, 1977).

Fascism

In 20th-century European history there was a fourth grand ideology present in the form of fascism, but it is most difficult to characterize in the terms being used. Like conservatism, it was a reaction to the modern world and an argument in favor of tradition. But like liberalism, it made use of modern technology to harness the state and, in the case of fascist Italy and Germany, to develop a complex military machine for conquests in the name of that ideology. The German movement even adopted the symbolism of socialism in its name—Nationalsozialistische Deutsche Arbeiterpartei—to designate its form of corporatist economic organization. Corporatism involves the organization of society into estates or corporate bodies, and, under fascism, these bodies are tightly controlled by the state.[1]

Like the preceding ideologies, fascism too was dependent on what went before, differing only in the lack of identification with any single socioeconomic segment of the society beyond its attraction to the disaffected (Hamilton, 1982; Maier, 1976, 506–521).

Nationalism

As we noted in Chapter 2, nationality is a way of categorizing people that builds on ties of kinship, making it an ascriptively derived characteristic. In its premodern or even early modern form, nation meant "an ethnically defined societal community" (Parsons, 1971, 87). It should then follow that nationalism is the ideology of nation or peoplehood—a set of beliefs emphasizing the special and separate character of a people, based on shared language, religion, or ethnicity. Such a definition appears deficient in describing efforts at nation building that deliberately seek to break with ascriptive ties in order to create a wider nationalism. Notable examples range from the United States as the "first new nation" (Lipset, 1963; Parsons, 1971, 87–94) to the many states emerging from colonial empires after World War II (e.g., Rupert Emerson, 1960). The initial definition proposed remains useful, however, in focusing attention on the continuing significance of kinship-derived cleavages. It is also appropriate for describing the underlying beliefs of nationalist movements concerned with the empowerment of ethnic groups without necessarily entailing their territorial separation.

In its original form, nationalism is an ancient ideology, often inseparable from religion, and long predating what have just been described as the grand ideologies of the modern world. Unlike them, it is limited in the ways it spells out explanations of events and goals for the future. That is, nationalism alone does not provide a blueprint for structuring a new nation beyond those issues that deal with the constitution of its peoplehood. Given this characteristic, along with great variations over time and by location, nationalism is less of an ideology than the grand ones previously outlined. Yet it remains an essential element in understanding the continuing political relevance of primary ascriptive ties and the importance these have for mobilizing people. As a rationale for political organization, nationalism goes along with low costs of governing where it encompasses linguistically, religiously, or ethnically homogeneous populations (Deutsch, 1966, 2–4).

Feminism

Like liberalism, conservatism, and socialism, feminism is an ideology of the modern world; like nationalism, it is a reminder of how earlier bases of cleavage remain powerful forces. The new forms in which the struggle for women's rights unfolds is itself a powerful argument for the sociologist to develop a historical consciousness, continually scanning messages from the past while anticipating future developments.

Modern feminism can trace its roots to the French Revolution, and the first systematic exposition of feminist ideals in England appeared in 1792 (Wollstonecraft, 1982). Women's participation in protest movements aimed at helping others has often been an avenue for stimulating their own consciousness. For example, in the United States, this progression took place as women worked to abolish slavery in the 19th century and then organized to gain their own suffrage (Randall, 1987, 208–209), and again as they supported civil rights in the 1960s and then organized for their own liberation (Freeman, 1975, 57–62). Today, no single statement of feminist ideology exists, varying by country and class and by scope and tactics (Randall, 1987). At the most general level, however, we can define feminism as a "political ideology which argues that men and women should have equal roles in society and that women have been denied support within the home and access to the marketplace because of discrimination and inadequate social institutions" (Klein, 1984, 2).

Connections

I have deliberately stressed the origins of these ideologies, not only to indicate their relation with social cleavages, but to remind us of how important they have been in fueling major political movements that have affected the course of history. The order in which the three grand ideologies of the modern world have been presented—liberalism, reflecting the aspirations of the new middle classes; conservatism, the reaction to modernism and the defense of the old ruling class; and socialism, the argument for reconstituting the position of the newly emerged working classes—is more than just a historical coincidence, since each is a reaction to the one or ones preceding it. In addition, each may crosscut other ideologies, as happens with nationalism and feminism.

In Chapter 3, one of the reasons given for the absence of a viable socialist party in the United States was the lack of feudalism as a component of the preexisting social structure to which socialism could react. Similarly, as a system of belief, socialism requires the prior existence of conservatism (Hartz, 1964, 69–122) because it shares with the latter an organic conception of society that is otherwise foreign to liberalism. An imaginative outgrowth of this argument is developed by G. Horowitz (1968) to account for the differences between the United States and Canada with respect to the existence of socialism. In Canada, the existence of a "tory touch" is sufficient to account for the subsequent growth of socialism. In the United States, the emigration or suppression of conservatives who opposed the revolution guaranteed that neither Burkean-style conservatism nor socialism would find congenial homes.

Some elaboration of the meaning of grand ideologies in the United States follows, bringing us to the present and paving the way to ask for the cues used by the ordinary person for making sense of an apparently bewildering political world. The answers that follow also serve to set apart the significance of grand ideologies.

THE U.S. SETTING

Conservatism

The uses of liberalism and conservatism in the 20th century, especially in the United States, have to be approached cautiously. A prime example of existing conceptual confusion is demonstrated from an interview granted by Jimmy Carter prior to his election to the presidency in 1976:

> On human rights, civil rights, environmental quality, I consider myself to be liberal. On the management of government, on openness of government, on strengthening individual liberties and local levels of government, I consider myself a conservative. And I don't see that the two attitudes are incompatible. (Carter, 1976, 81)

Writing more than two decades ago, Rossiter (1962) detected two themes in U.S. conservatism, one of which was quite close to the Burkean ideal type and found among Catholic intellectuals. Its concerns were with basic values like family solidarity and communal integrity, presaging the growth of this kind of conservatism and its special attraction to Catholic voters on such issues as abortion and pornography. This particular brand of conservatism has found a receptive home in the Republican Party and has been a drawing card for Catholics. Yet even today, when these moral issues are also overtly political ones, many Catholic voters still feel more comfortable in the Democratic Party.

The second, and older, thread of U.S. conservatism is of a different sort, opposing centralized government, governmental regulation, and anything perceived to interfere with the free market. Historically, conservatism in the United States has been associated with "rugged individualism," and, in its economic manifestations, it best resembles 19th-century liberalism. The economists of the University of Chicago, so often associated with the philosophy of free-market conservatism, are a variant of that liberalism.

Liberalism

If conservatives are really liberal, then what is a liberal in the United States? Probably liberalism's greatest appearance of consistency came about through the New Deal. While, in fact, it was a highly piecemeal and pragmatic approach to political problems, the New Deal affected the definition of liberalism by associating it with centralized government, governmental responsibility for social welfare, and some governmental participation in the economy. Though this kind of modest statism is often perceived as a liberal counterpart of economic conservatism, in its bare outlines it does not suggest a particular position on civil rights or civil liberties, and certainly not on foreign policy.

The premise that liberalism was associated with the strongest support for civil liberties and civil rights probably was most overt during the 1960s. But that was also a period when the whole meaning of liberalism came into question. For those dismayed by the changes that occurred in that era, liberalism was the ideology of breakdown and disorder, little better than communism. For those who wanted more rapid social changes and were dissatisfied with U.S. international involvements and with the slow pace with which rights were accorded to blacks, liberalism was simply another form of conservatism (Martin, 1979, 191–254). Speaking at the antiwar march on Washington on October 27, 1965, Carl Oglesby, then president of Students for a Democratic Society (SDS), the main student-based organization of the time advocating participatory democracy, concluded his evaluation of the evils at home and abroad by admitting that "others will make of it that I sound mighty anti-American. To these I say: Don't blame *me* for that! Blame those who mouthed my liberal values and broke my American heart" (Oglesby, 1971, 21).

U.S. Radicalism

While there are existing concepts for describing political ideologies that propose radical changes in economic structures, with communism and socialism the best known, these concepts do not seem appropriate for the U.S. experience, and *radicalism* has become the more widely used term. It can be used as a more generic concept for subsuming movements like Populism (Hicks, 1961), an indigenous ideology for change that would localize power in the hands of farmers, as well as for the range of sectarian movements on the left (Howard, 1977). The concept of radicalism is needed to reflect such movements' commitment to redistribution of political power.

The quarrels between the old and new left over the international role of the United States and the relevance of deviant lifestyles provide, in hindsight, additional evidence of the individualistic, and even anarchistic, strains in U.S. political thinking. Despite efforts to reinterpret the relevance of Marx (Zinn, 1971, 36–48), the new left was too heterogeneous to live comfortably with a single ideology. Marx, to be sure, has long had followers in the United States, but this fact has not made Marxism the only, or even the dominant, ideology of U.S. radicalism.

The special meanings of U.S. radicalism are also evident in feminism and the movement for black power. According to Randall (1987, 6), radical feminism insists that "sex is the fundamental division in society to which all other differences, such as social class or race, are merely secondary" (Randall, 1987, 6). It represents an apparently more attractive alternative to Marxist feminism, which sees the subjugation of women in terms of a capitalist economy (Randall, 1987, 8). The radicalism of "'black nationalism,' involving rejection of white America as a reference group and a readiness to use any means necessary to promote black pride and black self-determination" (Killian, 1975, xvii), also retains its uniquely U.S. qualities, despite its identification with the anticolonialism of the Third World (Killian, 1975, 169–170).

IDEOLOGY IN EVERYDAY LIFE

Public Beliefs

There is a long-standing controversy in the United States over whether the general population possesses coherent and consistent frameworks for evaluating political events. The most influential work on the existence of ideology at the mass level was done by Philip Converse (1964). For Converse and his colleagues at the University of Michigan, ideology was understood as a set of consistent beliefs ranging along a single continuum from liberal to conservative, giving the latter concepts the same meanings they have had since their European origins. When responses of the U.S. adult population to questions about good and bad points of the two major parties and of the presidential candidates were subjected to these stringent conditions, only 2.5 percent of those sampled in 1956 could be identified as ideologues, and another 9 percent could be considered near-ideologues, since they used abstract concepts but without elaborating them. A further 48 percent responded in terms of group interests, for example, how well the parties helped specific groups. Twenty-four percent spoke of the goodness or badness of the times while the remaining replies were devoid of issue content.

This picture of "ideological innocence" (Kinder, 1983) was buttressed for Converse by historical evidence separating the beliefs of elites from the mass public. Further search for ideological thinking, even granting that the public did not use abstract categories to describe them, was made by analyzing responses to structured questions asked in 1956, 1958, and 1960. The results showed a low level of "issue constraint" in the sense of consistency among the responses or their stability over time. Converse concluded that whenever stable and consistent beliefs are found, they are the result of the personal salience of the issues in question and generally are limited to a minority of the population.

Needless to say, Converse has not gone unchallenged, with his critics concentrating either on methodological issues of question wording or historical ones of survey timing. Most prominent among those who argue that the U.S. voter has become more ideological are Nie, Verba, and Petrocik, and much of their argument hangs on the effects of changes in the wording of questions (Nie, Verba, and Petrocik, 1979, 1981). The considerable literature on this topic can be summarized in the conclusion reached by Kinder and Sears (1985, 668), that the "instability of public opinion cannot be reduced entirely to technical problems of measurement. Instability reflects both fuzzy measures *and* fuzzy citizens."

Effects of History

A somewhat different tack is taken by those who emphasize an apparent increase in ideological thinking as a function of timing. Pomper (1975) exemplifies this line of criticism, arguing that Converse was correct in his characterization of the U.S. public in the 1950s exactly because this was a period of low ideology. In the presidential elections of 1952 and 1956, when an immensely popular war hero, Dwight D. Eisenhower, ran against a former governor of Illinois, Adlai Stevenson, both the inclinations of President Eisenhower and the campaign strategies of the Republican Party coincided in downplaying partisan differences and emphasizing leadership and national unity. The result was that many people who had been inclined to the Democrats by social characteristics and even by past voting were drawn to the Eisenhower presidential campaign. They did not, however, necessarily change their political outlook. When John F. Kennedy ran against Richard Nixon, the main effect was to bring back into the Democratic fold some of the Catholic voters who had otherwise supported the Republicans. But real consistency in attitudes and voting increased more sharply in the presidential election of 1964, when Barry Goldwater ran an unusually ideological campaign, emphasizing his belief that what the voter was looking for was "a choice, not an echo." Though the outcome of that election appeared to refute Goldwater, in fact it presented an opportunity for voters to demonstrate a strong fit between their political views and their support of the Democratic presidential candidate.

Alternative Meaning Systems

It was the 1964 election that motivated much of the criticism of Converse, but, in some sense, it would be the last one to do so. The 1968 presidential election period was a more troubled one, when campus unrest, violence in the black ghettoes, and an unpopular war in Southeast Asia contributed to President Johnson's decision to refrain from seeking a second term. The election then pitted Vice-President Hubert H. Humphrey against Richard M. Nixon and provided an environment for a poor fit between the views of voters and their support for the presidential candidates. In 1972, the Democratic candidate, George McGovern, was like the mirror image of Barry Goldwater, emphasizing strong positions on issues, but succeeding only in raising doubts about his ability to lead the country. As a consequence, in both elections, some people with Democratically oriented attitudes voted for the Republican presidential candidate.

Whatever the importance attributed to the coincidence between historically specific issues, the responses of parties and leaders to them, and the attitudes of voters, there is still little in the argument about timing that speaks to underlying belief systems. For these we are better served by the research of someone like Robert Lane (1962), who interviewed 15 ordinary men in the late 1950s, asking them about their beliefs and outlooks. Lane defines ideology much as I have, as a set of more or less coherent beliefs for organizing and explaining political events. By his methods, combining issues of concern to political science with the techniques of psychotherapy, he revealed the beliefs arising out of the experiences these men had, especially with their families and on the job. Even though there were common elements, for example, in arguing that religion had no place in the day-to-day turmoil of politics, in expressions of uncertainty about the future, or in feelings of political alienation—the sense of having little effect on the conduct of politics—these beliefs generally existed in a disjointed way. While Lane argued that his procedures allowed one to uncover "the 'latent' ideologies of the common man" (Lane, 1962, 16), he also admitted that the men themselves were not inclined to put their ideas together into a coherent system (Kinder and Sears, 1985, 670). A later analysis of survey data responds to Lane's admission by demonstrating how, despite inconsistencies in individual attitudes, once they are aggregated into socially meaningful groups based on characteristics like class and gender, it is possible to speak of group beliefs (Feld and Grofman, 1988).

From the perspective of those who work with a Marxian framework, debates over survey results must also appear beside the point in establishing the existence of a popular ideology. For them, as for Marx, what is important is how workers create class consciousness from out of their life experiences. Though this process is empirically more difficult to document than would be the case if appropriate survey data were available, scholars in this tradition still distinguish between the ideology of common people and those of intellectuals. For example, based on a wide-ranging historical analysis of protests and revolutions, Rude (1980) considers the experiences of ordinary people the basis of "inherent ideology" in contrast to that expressed by intellectuals—"derived ideology." If the political beliefs of ordinary people begin with personal assessments, as Lane documents, they still are politically relevant because they derive from more generalizable social experiences. As a result, these beliefs have the potential for mobilizing collective action by becoming linked to more elaborate ideologies (see Roy, 1984, 502–503, for a review of relevant studies). It is in this sense, as with blacks and women, that the previously unmobilized can come to see that "the personal is political" (Randall, 1987, 12).

It is futile to look for the presence of grand ideologies among the majority of the public when even the meaning of those ideologies has become ambiguous. Yet, granting that futility, Wildavsky (1987) still delivered a presidential address to the American Political Science Association that was a plea for acknowledging the importance of general belief systems, linking individuals with their society's culture. With culture providing the boundary within which political meanings are organized, he argued that it is possible to find a small number of underlying themes. In the United States, these revolve on attachments to individualism, but ones that distinguish ''egalitarian collectivism''—involving preference for equality of results—from ''competitive individualism''—preference for equality of opportunity.

Working with different evidence and coming from a different disciplinary perspective, Kinder and Sears (1985, 674–676) also see ''tantalizing'' evidence that there are a small number of critical values used for organizing political meaning, but they conclude that it is still too early to say whether these are truly central. That is, what remains unsettled is whether the interpretative schemes most people use at least some of the time can be treated as sufficiently coherent and few in number to be analogous to grand ideologies. Moreover, we will still need to consider how they relate to the major social cleavages.

SPREADING THE WORD

Literacy

Recent interest in the culture of organizations (Frost et al., 1985) is a recognition that organization means the establishment of customary ways of acting and that these, in turn, become associated with beliefs about the appropriateness of chosen behavior. In other words, the culture of an organization is the means of reducing randomness. One important way of breaking out of established ways—that is, starting a revolution—is through the creation of a new system of values. Consolidation of those values into an ideology requires that ideas be put into a form accessible to others. Revolutions, it is true, may not be caused by ideologies, nor need ideologies be the main impetus to the way they develop popular support. Yet without some organizing ideas, even if held by only a small group in the initial stages, there can be no revolution. In this sense, the revolutionary idea is more important than the revolutionary leader, no matter how charismatic. It is more important because it can acquire a life of its own, removed from the original promulgators, the original conditions out of which it arose, or the time and place of its origin. But in order for ideology to acquire this independent existence, it has to be present in written form.

Just as controversies exist over the role of ideas or ideology in the development and spread of significant social movements, so too does controversy continue over the importance of literacy in enabling people to read about such ideas. Most convincing is the view that literacy changes the thought patterns of a society (Goody, 1968). In the case of the French Revolution, Markoff (1986) provides information about the effects of literacy on the likelihood of being mobilized to the ideas of the revolution. In less literate rural France, the kinds of uprisings that occurred were more likely to be in response to rumors of outside invasion. In more literate areas, however, uprisings were directed against the central social institutions of the old system of authority. While it is true that evidence of this sort is indirect, it fits with what was said in Chapter 3, for example, on the importance of having the Bible in the vernacular for setting the stage to spread political messages.

Mass Media

In the United States, there is generally much less interest in literacy (Graff, 1986) than in the political effects of the mass media. The landmark study of the latter was by Lazarsfeld, Berelson, and Gaudet (1944) in Erie County. They began with the assumption that radio, the main source of information for voters house-bound by the depression and used with great skill in his "fireside chats" by President Roosevelt, would be an important influence in creating Democratic voting choices. The print media, controlled by Republican owners, would influence those who read them regularly in a Republican direction. These predictions were not met, since, from the outset of the campaign, the largest share of the electorate was already committed to its partisan choice. Yet, over the years, researchers have continued their search for the ability of the mass media to change people's minds (Roberts and Maccoby, 1985, 540). Only recently has there been sufficient atten-tion to studying the effects of the media more broadly, covering the impact of special circumstances and particular audiences and the relation to agenda setting. (For a summary, see Roberts and Maccoby, 1985.) For example, Lang and Lang (1983) recount how the media, and especially television, made the public aware of the Watergate break-in and its tie-in with the White House and continued to play an active role in shaping the way both government and the public responded to the crisis.

The mass media enable ideology to be spread at a pace and on a scale not otherwise possible. They do so, to a limited extent, merely by acting as means of communication. The process is confounded by the fact that television in particular is a principal medium of entertainment, contaminating, in a sense, every subject that it presents. Using a combination of experimental studies with survey data, Iyengar and Kinder (1987) conclude, as do other observers, that television news affects our assessment of what is important. In addition, by regularly making some messages more accessible, the news "sets the terms by which political judgments are ren-dered and political choices made" (Iyengar and Kinder, 1987, 4).

The mass media play an even more significant role when they have been directly captured by the sponsors of the ideology, as occurs in totalitarian states. Those who see the media as "cultivating entire belief systems" (Roberts and Maccoby, 1985, 580–582) do not limit their conclusions to such states but argue that the mass media, even in democratic societies, serve the interests of dominant groups and shape world views accordingly. Taking this argument further, Noelle-Neumann (1984) sees a wider "spiral of silence," in which unpopular minority views are kept from expression.

Alternative Communication Links

Wildavsky is correct that shared norms and values grow out of social experiences, and at least some of these are relevant to politics. We can also assume that such cultural elements are communicated and spread through the normal process of socialization, mentioned in Chapter 2 in regard to the way partisan identification is likely to be passed on. That is, formative experiences in home, school, work, the military, and so on provide the milieus in which beliefs are grounded. Socializing experiences are the means by which group loyalties are formed. Evidence of their manifestation is provided in the work of Converse, cited earlier, where the largest category of responses in evaluating parties and candidates consisted of group-related concerns rather than traditionally ideological ones. Another perspective comes from the work of Sears and his associates. They argue that responses to political issues are shaped by "symbolic politics," by which they mean attachments to party, traditional ideological leanings, and racism—themselves all rooted in group experiences. That is, "demographic measures . . . describe social background, and hence the socialization origins of symbolic attitudes" (Sears et al., 1980, 677). If the host of socializing agents are important for shaping values with implications for interpreting the political world, we should not overlook the possibility that those same agents will attempt to inculcate ideologies deliberately. Such indoctrination happens, for example, when the goal of a school system is to teach a partisan version of citizenship.

By the same token, we should not assume that grand ideologies are solely communicated through the mass media, including print. For example, the Social Credit Party in the Canadian province of Alberta, based on the monetary teachings of a British engineer, Major Clifford Hugh Douglas, spread its original message through the use of small study groups, including ones that had initially been set up to promote the ideals of another ideological movement, the United Farmers of Alberta, and supplemented by others tied to religious evangelism (Macpherson, 1962, 144–145; Irving, 1959, 50–53). The Social Credit experience illustrates how cell-like organizations, described in Chapter 3, serve not only to promote the growth of particular kinds of movements, but also, through the face-to-face communication they entail, to provide the ideal milieu for studying the written text of an ideological master.

THE IMPACT OF IDEOLOGY

"The End of Ideology"

Ideologies are important because they serve as the basis of existing political organizations, the means of differentiating political parties and movements, and instruments for mobilizing popular support to fight and even die for a cause. An assessment of the impact of ideology needs to differentiate the beliefs of the ordinary person from the ideology of elites who begin with an overriding commitment to a set of programmatic goals and, when successful, end with the resources to ensure that others follow their policies, whether or not they fully believe in them. Our concern with ordinary people should not blind us to the way in which ideology is much more than just a tool for mass mobilization. Certainly it plays this role, and it does so most effectively where there is an aggrieved population and effective means for communicating with them. But the historically significant ideology arises when the actions it sets in motion are able to accomplish the goals advocated. Only then does the authority structure, legitimated by the ideology and augmented by a whole range of resources, including the use of force, ensure that its vision of the world becomes the dominant one.

Writers in the 1950s and early 1960s, of whom one of the best known was Daniel Bell (1962), were inclined to prophecy the "end of ideology." It did not take long for this position to be attacked both in the United States and the rest of the world. Reviewing the controversy generated by the work of Bell and others, including himself, Lipset (1981, 524–565) now argues that their intent was to predict the demise of total, all-encompassing ideologies and their connection with the cleavage structure of society. Specifically, it was not the end of socialism, or of class conflict, or even of class consciousness that was expected, but the coincidence of all three into a volatile whole. The ideological dispositions of intellectuals or students were not at issue:

> Efforts to find a mass base, beyond an affluent minority of the intelligentsia, on the part of New Left groups which reject the established Social Democratic, Communist, and Democratic parties, all oriented to the electoral system, have failed dramatically in areas as diverse as France, Germany, Italy, Northern Europe, and the United States. The vast majority of American New Leftists, including some of their most prominent spokespersons, have joined the Democratic Party in the United States, finding sufficient ideological sustenance in the liberal and populist positions that have been identified with George McGovern and Edward Kennedy. (Lipset, 1981, 564)

What Lipset, in effect, is saying is that the expectation of strong commitment to a grand ideology at a mass level no longer describes the political world of great majorities in the Western world, assuming it ever did. Elsewhere, expectations are different. For new nations to find their way through a "forest of problems without any ideological guidance at all seems impossible," as Geertz (1973, 229) observed, and there the ideologies may begin with students or intellectuals, but they will likely affect many others.

Ideology in the University

If students can be expected to remain open to ideological appeals, under what conditions might ideology breach the structural barriers and channel student discontent against the university? Even though UIC students can conceive of the university as a political system and share enough experiences in dealing with the university administration to come up with similar explanations of how things work, the only result is individually articulated sentiments without guidance for collective action. There is insufficient stimulus to action in such systems of meaning, which are analogous to what Lane found for his "common men." We need to look elsewhere for examples of mobilizing ideologies, and one place to find the kind of ideology needed to enlist student support is in the experiences of the University of California–Berkeley Free Speech Movement (FSM).

The immediate stimulus to the emergence of the FSM was a decision by the University of California administration, in September 1964, to enforce its control over a strip of land that had previously been considered part of the city of Berkeley. The area had been used for political activities otherwise not permitted on the campus. This was a period when the civil rights movement was active in the Bay area, as well as on the Berkeley campus, and its presence provided the external forces that could combine with those internal to the university to produce a student strike. The incendiary role of the administration occurred in a setting that had been smoldering for some time.

> The student revolt of the fall of 1964 seems less like a sudden and surprising explosion from within the body politic of the university, but rather the natural outgrowth of eight years of expanding student political involvement, and of an increasing conflict over the proper limits of student rights to express their views, listen to the views of others, and finally take action for the causes they favor. (Heirich and Kaplan, 1965, 34–35)

The repressive role of the university on the particular issue of free speech became a starting point for a more inclusive ideology, conceiving the university as a factory for the exploitation of students. On the one side stood the university:

> In contrast to this tendency to separate the issues, many thousands of *us,* the Free Speech Movement, have asserted that politics and education are inseparable, that the *political* issue of the First and Fourteenth Amendments and the *educational issue* cannot be separated. In place of "great university" we have said "impersonal bureaucracy," "machine," or "knowledge factory." If we emerge as victors from our long and still hard-to-be-won battle for free speech, will we then be returning to *less* than a factory? *Is* this a great university? If we are to take *ourselves* seriously we must define precisely what we meant when we said "knowledge factory." (Free Speech Movement, 1965, 211)

On the other side were the students:

> At present in the United States, students—middle class youth—are the major exploited class. The labor of intelligent youth *is* needed, and they are accordingly subjected to tight scheduling, speedup, and other factory exploitative methods. Then it is not surprising if they organize their CIO. It is frivolous to tell them to go elsewhere if they don't like the rules, for they have no choice but to go to college, and one factory is like another. (Free Speech Movement, 1965, 208)

Mobilized students paralyzed the Berkeley campus for six months and set a model for student activism elsewhere for the next several years. Given today's circumstances, there seems little prospect for the development of a comparable ideology of student protest centered on the university. But having said that, there are still more difficult questions about the role of ideology that are left unanswered. Looking back after two decades, there seems no way to evaluate how much weight ideology played in mobilizing students. Nor do we know, despite all their pamphlets and speeches, if students were able to budge Berkeley even slightly from being a "knowledge factory" to moving in the direction of a humane, responsive educational setting.

NOTE

1. In the syndicalist variant, power is decentralized and the organization of factories is under worker control. Liberal democratic corporatism gives a policy-making role to business and labor in conjunction with government (Schmitter, 1974).

CHAPTER 5

THE ROLE
OF THE STATE

INTRODUCTION

Sociologists are able to find politics in any stable relationship involving two or more people. Since an organized state is not necessary for dealing with political problems, some sociologists may have tended to neglect roles played by the state. But if neglect occurred, it was not simply an oversight. Decisions about whether or not to include the state in sociological analyses of politics have been affected by extensive controversies over the relation between society and state and over the most appropriate way of defining the state.

How the state is defined has an impact on the kinds of activities and relationships that become subject to sociological analysis. If the state is considered only in the form of centralized agencies of governance and control, we have no way of assimilating studies of local communities. By including British and U.S. variants of attention to the urban political world, broader questions are raised about the nature of the state.

Once the state is present, there is a presumption that new kinds of effects on the society and its members are produced. Some commentators see these largely in terms of crises that can only be resolved through revolution. In general, the clearest argument for state impact lies in analyses of policymaking.

This volume ends with some instances of how the state affects the everyday life of its citizens. These examples do not bring us, in a full circle, to a satisfactory conclusion because, as the state grows in influence, the lines between state and society are again unclear.

SOCIOLOGICAL CONCERNS

Sociology and Politics

Giovanni Sartori, a political scientist with a stake in differentiating the sociologist's concern with politics from the political scientist's, defined what he felt would be a more precise "political sociology" by reaching the following conclusion:

> In actuality much of what goes under the misnomer of "political sociology" is nothing more than a sociology of politics ignorant of political science; in substance, an exploration of the polity that sets aside as "givens" the variables of the political scientist. (Sartori, 1969, 69)

Sartori would be quite unimpressed with my initial premise, presented in Chapter 1 and quite unexceptional for a sociologist, that every social system faces political problems. By this I meant that any ongoing relationship will require that decisions be made with consequences for everyone involved in the relationship; those decisions are specifically political when they are concerned with regulating the distribution of what is collectively valued. It was in this sense that I justified speaking of the "politics of everyday life."

Sartori, we can assume, would be equally disparaging of the logic of this volume, where I began by looking for the roots of political organization and conflict in the cleavage structure of a society. He finds little to be gained from attention to the societal underpinnings of political behavior or from concern for the society generally. Racial cleavages, described in Chapter 2, and the differential manner in which whites and blacks were mobilized in the southern states of the United States, described in Chapter 3, would be, in his terms, trivial compared to the explanatory power of state regulation of voter registration (prior to changes in voting rights in the 1960s) in accounting for differences in voter turnout for whites and blacks. Certainly the effects of voter registration laws have been profound (e.g., Kelley, Ayres, and Bowen, 1967), but such barriers to mobilization are, for us, still only part of the picture.

Similarly, in Chapter 2, while I spoke of the potential of social cleavages to become politicized, I gave no explicit examples of how the state might be involved in the process of their politicization. In contrast, Laitin (1985, 285–316), a political scientist, answers the puzzling question of why religious cleavages have not become the basis of political conflict in the Yoruba region of modern Nigeria by reaching back to colonial experience. Under the British practice of "indirect rule" (Lugard, 1922), traditional rulers were buttressed, ensuring their loyalty, and leaving colonial authorities free to carry out overseeing functions. For most of the indigenous population, when there were contacts with authority, they would be with traditional rulers. This encouraged identification with those communal ties associated with ancestral cities. These ties, while originally stimulated by the imperial state, became sufficiently institutionalized into Yoruba political life to continue to suppress the political relevance of religious cleavages even after independence.

The preceding examples demonstrate that attention to consequences of state actions are obviously valuable, in defense of Sartori. But just as political science does not supersede the contributions of sociology, so concern with the effects of the state does not eliminate the need to consider social effects on politics as well.

Sartori's complaint implies that sociologists do not pay direct attention to the institutions, organizations, or systems of authority associated with governing; or to the consequences of the acts, decisions, and operations emanating from government, either for members of the polity or for relations with other polities. In a form more in keeping with sociology, his perspective appears to underlie Skocpol's argument for "bringing the state back in."

> The meanings of public life and the collective forms through which groups become aware of political goals and work to attain them arise, not from societies alone, but at the meeting points of states and societies. Consequently, the formation, let alone the political capacities, of such apparently purely socioeconomic phenomena as interest groups and classes depends in significant measure on the structures and activities of the very states the social actors, in turn, seek to influence. (Skocpol, 1985, 27)

Let us agree, then, that the state is a subject important for the sociologist's study.

State and Society

While every social system may also be a miniature polity, not every one will develop a state. This is true even when the social system in question encompasses an entire society. The distinction between state and society is seen by Alford and Friedland as a problem in theorizing, dividing social scientists according to whether they see the state as an "entity" or a "relation."

> If the state is an entity, with legal authority and a monopoly on legal violence, then one can legitimately refer to public and private spheres and distinguish among the state, the economy, and culture. This language presupposes the existence of the state as a separate set of institutions, organizations, or functions, which are affected by interest groups, elites, or class agents. (Alford and Friedland, 1985, 26)

When the state is conceived as a relation, even if it is accorded some autonomy, it expresses "values, interests, and imperatives that cannot be understood in any meaningful way except as part of the whole society" (Alford and Friedland, 1985, 26). We should sense from their distinction the tendentiousness that is characteristic of discussions of state-society relations, and, while Alford and Friedland do little to resolve disputes—probably an impossible task—they are helpful in highlighting the fundamental issues of defining the state and accounting for its autonomy.

Today, writers on the state converge on two themes—the state as a historically specific entity and its distinctness from government:

> The modern concept of state was formed during the period from the thirteenth to the sixteenth centuries and represented a decisive shift away from the idea of the ruler maintaining his state to the notion of a separate legal and constitutional order—the state—which the ruler had an obligation to maintain. (Alford and Friedland, 1985, 1)

Bendix (1978) used this transformation from personal rule to peoplehood to account for nation-building as it took shape in 16th-century Western Europe. More than just a change in type of government was involved, however. If we follow Alford and Friedland's approach, statehood implies "not merely the specific regime in power at any one moment—the governing coalition of political leaders—but also the basis for a regime's authority, legality, and claim for popular support" (Alford and Friedland, 1985, 1).

At the heart of the debate about state-society relations is the independence of the former:

> States conceived as organizations claiming control over territories and people may formulate and pursue goals that are not simply reflective of the demands or interests of social groups, classes, or society. This is what is meant by "state autonomy." (Skocpol, 1985, 9)

But while such autonomy is crucial in allowing us to treat the state as an independent actor, it is also central to why the state remains such a troublesome concept to sociologists (e.g., Thomas and Meyer, 1984).

Although Alford and Friedland attribute a relational treatment of the state solely to "pluralists"—those who emphasize the social underpinnings of political behavior and the impact of that behavior on government but take the structures of government for granted—it is a perspective that has had more general currency, at least among non-Marxist sociologists (Poggi, 1978, ix–x). Nevertheless, many sociologists of this mainstream perspective appear to have adapted to the need for viewing the state as an autonomous actor. They include Parsons (1971), who treated the state as the culmination of an evolutionary process of differentiation. Bendix (1964, 1968, 1978) deals with such issues as the break with feudalism represented by kingship and the transition to the modern state, in which the complex functions of governing are monopolized. Within the state, the creation of citizenship becomes a means of regularizing relations with individuals and groups who come under its control. From a quite different starting point, Coleman (1974), who sees unequal power struggles between individuals and corporate actors, assigns ultimate controlling power to the state.

Badie and Birnbaum (1983, 3–11) try to argue that Marx himself recognized an important role for the state, but in the end they are forced to conclude that he saw it merely as an adjunct of capitalism, captured in the statement, "The executive of the modern state is but a committee for managing the common affairs of the whole bourgeoisie" (Marx and Engels, 1959, 9). Marxists remain caught up by the underlying argument of their intellectual heritage, in which economic factors of production determine the nature of society, relegating the organs of government to the superstructure. So Miliband (1977, 90–91), while outlining four functions performed by all states, notes that their performance will inevitably be done in ways that perpetuate the dominant societal interests—"The intervention of the state is always and necessarily partisan." But if the state is only shaped by class interests, then Marxists must remain constrained in what they can expect from state actions (Skocpol, 1985, 5).

Defining the State

Poggi views the modern state as a complex of norms regulating occupants of governmental office for the purpose of "rule" (Poggi, 1978, 1) and specifies its character in terms of the unity of the 19th-century state.

> There is the unity of the state's territory, which comes to be bounded as much as possible by a continuous geographical frontier that is militarily defensible. There is a single currency and a unified fiscal system. Generally, there is a single "national" language. . . . Finally, there is a unified legal system that allows alternative juridical traditions to maintain validity only in peripheral areas and for limited purposes. (Poggi, 1978, 93)

Other definitions of the state emphasize its centralized character (for example, Tilly, 1975, 70), but these are less useful because centralization appears to be both historically and culturally more circumscribed than are the factors specified by Poggi. Some of the reasons for varying definitions of the state are attributable to different perspectives on its origin, of which two are basic, though not totally opposed.

One approach, compatible with the Durkheimean emphasis on the universal movement toward increased division of labor, sees the state emerging as part of an evolutionary process in which the growth of differentiated social organization is manifested through the separation of political institutions and related organizations from other aspects of the society (Parsons, 1966). In this perspective, evolutionary change is adaptive, increasing the capacity of a society to survive because the state provides it with enhanced rationality (Orum, 1989, 99). The alternative approach is often not totally antievolutionary but differs in putting the weight of explanation on the side of historically unique sets of factors rather than on inevitable developmental change.

Conceiving the state as an evolutionary adaptation to an increasingly complex world fits well with those theories of modernization that argue that, as societies became industrialized, their states would acquire liberal democratic forms (Lipset, 1981, 27–63; Dahl, 1971). But such theories have also been criticized on grounds that they do a poor job in explaining the undemocratic character of regimes in both advanced capitalist and newly emerging states. In reviewing the empirical research on this subject, Jackman's conclusion is as follows:

> While economic development may lead to increased political democracy at earlier stages of industrialization, a threshold is reached at later stages of this process beyond which the effects of economic development on political democracy become progressively weaker. (Jackman, 1975, 84)

The evolutionary basis of the original argument is directly attacked by those who see gaps in economic development as the result of exploitation by more highly developed states (e.g., Frank, 1967).

Without taking a directly evolutionary position, the increasing rationality of the modern state was an overarching theme in the work of Max Weber, whom Badie and Birnbaum (1983, 17) consider the true father of the sociological study of politics. For Weber, rationality was both a form of social organization and a cultural characteristic of Western society. It underlies the emergence and growth of bureaucracy, which, more than anything else, is the hallmark of the modern world. Perhaps the grimmest elaboration of Weber's world view was made by Mills (1956) when he postulated three powerful organizations in U.S. society—corporate, military, and the political executive. He argued that each had become centralized and interrelated, resulting in the appearance of a national power elite made up of a relatively small number of men in these organizations' top positions. Today, however, equating the state with a small number of individuals, regardless of how critically placed they may be, does not appear to be a useful solution to the problem of how the state should be defined.

The distinction between public and private spheres of social action first acquired meaning in Western history when secular powers were successful in attaining separation from the religious realm (Poggi, 1978, 120). In earlier chapters I made reference to such developments in Tudor England and the Germanic states at the time of Luther. But since the full flowering of the modern state occurred simultaneously with that of capitalism, many have traced a causal connection between the two, especially those neo-Marxists who relate the crises of the modern state with the internal contradictions of capitalism (Jessop, 1982, 78–141). In contrast, we are indebted to Weber (1958) for noting the independence of capitalism from the state. In *The Protestant Ethic and the Spirit of Capitalism* he observed how capitalism contributed to the development of England without a concomitant growth in the administrative agencies of the central state.

Evolutionary stages of development and historical specificity combine in those theories that find the origin of the modern state in the breakdown of feudalism. For example, Anderson (1974) argues that absolute monarchies emerged in 16th-century England, France, and Spain along with standing armies, a permanent bureaucracy, a system of national taxation and law, and the beginnings of a market economy at the same time as feudal relations continued in rural areas. While he is most concerned with how these changes heralded the transition to capitalism, the changes themselves are important in indicating why some features of a modern centralized state could coexist with the dominance of a feudal aristocracy. Like Marx, Anderson presents a theory of change that sees evolution operating until there is a buildup of inner contradictions that can only be resolved through revolution. Equally important to his argument is the simultaneous presence of these conditions in only some parts of Europe, giving further evidence that change is neither uniform nor inevitable.

A simple, unilinear evolutionary perspective is inadequate to account for contemporaneous differences in modern states; yet increased social differentiation is a critical stimulant to their emergence. Badie and Birnbaum touch base with these and other competing theories in arriving at their own evaluation.

> The state was a product neither of the rise of capitalism nor of the opening of new trade routes, let alone of the growth of industry. The state was not a mere effect of economic modernization, as many sociologists still argue. A more correct characterization would be the following: the state was the political response that some European societies were forced to make to an increasing division of labor coupled with strong resistance to social change on the part of certain elements of feudal society; it was a way of reconciling the growing political incapacity of the great lords with the fact that they still maintained substantial control over economic and social life. (Badie and Birnbaum, 1983, 135)

Where feudalism was strongest, the conditions were set for the emergence of the strongest forms of centralized state. It is in such conditions that we begin to see the special nature of Britain and the United States. In the former, feudalism was relatively weak; in the latter, it was absent.

THE ANGLO-AMERICAN EXPERIENCE

The experiences of Britain and the United States have to be dealt with separately because their historical development has helped create an intellectual climate that affects the treatment of the state. That is, it is understandable that social scientists in those countries have not been in the forefront of students of the state, given that both societies are characterized by relatively weak states (Badie and Birnbaum, 1983, 103). Weakness is a relative term and refers only to internal structures, not to external relations.[1]

It has been said that the average Englishman could live his life, at least up until the early 20th century, without any conscious awareness of how he was affected by the central state. This is implicitly a comparative statement, in which Britain is contrasted with continental European states, particularly France. The idea of the state as differentiated, autonomous, universalistic, and institutionalized (Badie and Birnbaum, 1983, 60) is premised on the rationalization of social existence, which becomes the means for consolidating power in the hands of a centralized administrative apparatus. The concept of nation-state is, in these terms, not a universally applicable concept but an Anglo-American invention, linking the peoplehood of a nation with the governing qualities of the state:

> The state was a French reaction against feudalism inspired by Roman culture, whereas the nation was an idea based on contract that originated in England, where social integration was never a real problem and the cultural influence of Protestantism was strong. (Badie and Birnbaum, 1983, 93)

Note that reference is to relatively homogeneous England, not to multiethnic Britain.

The weak state is manifested in reliance on local government and authority, including in the latter community leaders and interests that are able to carry out activities on behalf of the larger community. In adopting Badie and Birnbaum's distinction between weak and strong states I recognize that not everyone finds it convincing or agrees that local government forms part of the state (e.g., Thomas and Meyer, 1984, 463).

Local Government

The primacy of local authority has been long institutionalized in Britain, reflected in numerous studies of local government (e.g., Birch, 1959; Jones, 1969; Elcock, 1982). While the British Labour Party (BLP) has often been prominently represented in city councils, the political left has still displayed a notable ambivalence toward local government. On the one hand, the reorganization of local government in the 1970s was seen as a way of reducing working-class influence at that level (Dearlove, 1979; King, 1986, 183). On the other hand, the rationale for disregarding the local level lies in the BLP's concern for a strong central government to carry out programs that will affect all parts of the country (King, 1986, 167; Bassett, 1984). But there are also suggestions that views of local government are conditioned by which party is in power, with local autonomy receiving greatest support from the BLP when it is out of office (King, 1986, 184).

Evidence of "the relative non-involvement of trade unions in local issues, despite the growth of the public sector unions" (King, 1986, 178), is indicative of the need to take into account the kinds of interests mobilized to influence local government. Studies of local communities such as those of Croyden (Saunders, 1979), Kensington, and Chelsea (Dearlove, 1973) deal with the extent to which homeowners rather than tenants have greater impact on council decisions and how national business interests are often better served than local ones, even though the latter predominate on the councils. The last finding is part of the evidence of how national factors increasingly affect local issues even in the context of a relatively weak state. Some of these may be state directed, like the policy decisions of the central government, and others may be structural, like the movement of capital (King, 1986, 173–174). But whatever their source, they combine with the older concern with local government to stimulate approaches to relations with the state that are responsive to the history and culture of Britain.

As the previous paragraph has already suggested, one approach to local government takes account of the move to a more nationalized politics. Dunleavy's (1981) study of high-rise housing decisions is an example of how the central state

has increased its power over local issues. In addition, a new emphasis on profes-
sionalism has also added to the national scope of the state and the interest groups
with which it deals (King, 1986, 188–190).

Attention to interest groups, meanwhile, has led to applications of corporatism to British politics. Corporatism, to which we gave passing mention in the
discussion of major ideologies in Chapter 4, has ideologically left and right and
democratic and totalitarian variants.

> Both left and right derived corporatist solutions from medieval notions of separate
> industrial or economic corporations, with the former inclining towards syndicalist or
> guild socialist notions of more local forms of self-governance, and the latter finding
> extreme expression in fascist notions of a strong, hierarchically-ordered, state-disci-
> plined society in which large scale corporations would be formly [sic] wedded to
> national goals. (King, 1986, 119)

Corporatist elements in British government were first evident during World War I,
when organized economic groups, particularly the British Employers Confederation
and the Trades Union Congress, cooperated in organizing a wartime economy
(King, 1986, 118–120). At the local level, corporatist arguments see the state
involved in mobilizing interest groups and enlisting their help in policymaking
(King, 1986, 136–138, 185–188). In this perspective, the political participation of
organized interest groups is not simply a matter of their efforts to influence or
control government; rather, it is an aspect of deliberate state policy to incorporate
them (King, 1986, 185–188).

In the foregoing, reference to the state is local and distinct from the central
organs of government. This distinction allows conceiving of different kinds of states
within a single society, each at least partly autonomous because each has its own
organizations, functions, characteristic activities, and underlying principles (King,
1986, 180–185). This theory of the "dual state" (Cawson and Saunders, 1983)
builds on Castells's (1977, 460–461) distinction about the role of the urban state in
providing for collective consumption through the services it offers. The ultimate
value of this theory will depend on its usefulness but, at this time, one conclusion
may be drawn:

> Dual-state theory seems to have great explanatory potential for recent attempts by
> central governments in many western economies to circumscribe the financial power
> of local authorities and control levels of collective consumption that threaten both the
> fiscal base of government and the profitability of capital. (King, 1986, 184)

Local Power Elites

The English pattern of local authority was part of the heritage brought by
colonists to British North America, persisting through the unsettled time of the
Revolution and lasting into this century. Tocqueville's (1945, I, 62) observations,
made in 1831, about the "naturalness" of township government and the remoteness
of the federal government were characteristics of the American polity until probably

the New Deal. But even today the structure of the state in the United States guarantees its weakness.

> The key characteristic . . . is that power is fragmented and decentralized. The American state—those institutions and roles that are relatively insulated from particularistic pressures and concerned with general goals (primarily the White House and the State Department and to a lesser extent the Treasury and Defense Departments)—is weak in relation to its own society. . . . The potential international power of the state—the ability of central decision makers to change the behavior of other international actors and to provide collective goods for the international system if *all* of the society's resources could be used for state purposes (that is, if there are no domestic constraints)—is great. But the actual power of the state—the power resulting from the resources that central decision makers can actually extract from their own society—is much less. The difference between the two is probably larger for the United States than for any other advanced industrial society. (Krasner, 1978, 53)

The impact of these characteristics on the social sciences had been to direct attention to the local scene, leading not to concern with local government, as in Britain, but to concern with local community power. The underlying quest of numerous studies in this genre (for a summary, see Hawley and Wirt, 1968) was a determination of who is in charge. A leading representative is Hunter's (1963) study of Atlanta in the early 1950s. His concern was with people reputed to wield power, found by first developing lists of those "in prominent positions in four groups that may be assumed to have power connections. These groups were identified with business, government, civic associations, and 'society' activities" (Hunter, 1963, 11). From these lists, 40 names were identified by community judges who ranked the most influential and also responded to the question of who was the "top leader" (Hunter, 1963, 263). Leaders identified in this manner, and particularly the top leaders, had many characteristics in common—social clubs, residential area, prominence in the business world. "They are persons of dominance, prestige, and influence. They are, in part, the decision-makers for the total community" (Hunter, 1963, 24).

The notion of a single power elite, identifiable through its members' community reputation, produced both many similar studies and severe criticisms. Objecting both to Hunter's conclusion about the presence of a community power elite and Mills's (1956) conclusion about a national power elite, Dahl (1961) studied New Haven, Connecticut, where he focused on a number of critical issues that the community faced and then determined the identity of those involved in related decisions. His conclusion was that there was no single power elite but groups of powerful people associated with particular issues. Perhaps because Dahl is a political scientist, he also attributed much more significance to the office of mayor (Dahl, 1961, 183).

The ensuing debates between elitists (following Hunter) and pluralists (following Dahl) may obscure some essential agreements between the two. Despite real differences in method and theory (and hence in findings), they come together in conceiving of power as an attribute of a limited number of individuals that is openly exercised. But, above all, they agree that what goes on in urban settings is of consequence. Since then, there has been considerable rethinking of the consequential nature of urban politics in ways similar to what occurred in Britain, though with less overt state-centered theorizing.

Under the stimulus of the Johnson administration's urban policies, which produced a more nationalized government, there came to be a recognition of the limited roles available to city politicians and interest groups, similar to the British perspective on the subordination of the city to the central state.

> The place of the city within the larger political economy of the nation fundamentally affects the policy choices that cities make. In making these decisions, cities select those policies which are in the interests of the city, taken as a whole. It is these city interests, not the internal struggles for power within cities, that limit city policies and condition what local governments do. (Peterson, 1981, 4)

Skocpol's observations about New Haven also suggest the possibilities of limited initiative available to cities:

> In the classic pluralist studies of New Haven politics, Mayor Richard Lee's strong individual initiatives for urban renewal were extensively documented but not grounded in any overall state-centered analysis of the potential for certain kinds of mayors to make new uses of federal funding. (Skocpol, 1985, 4)

While the concept of the dual state does not appear in U.S. studies, it could be applied to those works that consider the autonomous activities of local communities, separate from whatever limits may be imposed on them by the central state. James (1988) gives an example of what can be done in this regard by comparing differences in voter registration by race in 575 counties in seven southern states. Despite federally mandated drives to increase black voter registration, differences remained as a result of local conditions. James's (1988, 205) variables are primarily tied to the class structure of each county, which he sees as determining the nature of the local state, including the identity of its officials and its resources. The fact that the local state can be treated as autonomous from the national one further suggests that analyses of the United States and other federal systems need to incorporate a sociological theory of federalism (for an example, see Engelmann and Schwartz, 1981, 81–82).

CRISES AND CHANGE

The State in Crisis

Even more than the concept of society, the concept of the state is inherently ambiguous and open to a variety of perspectives and analyses, as Alford and Friedland (1985) have so painstakingly demonstrated. Yet regardless of theoretical orientation, concern with the state seems frequently tied to perceptions of crises.

From the point of view of Marxists, the crisis of the state is inherent in capitalism, but it also stems from efforts to mitigate capitalism's failures through social welfare measures. For example:

> The world capitalist crisis, emerging from the tumultuous 1960s, heralds the decline of the welfare State—of the "solution" to the previous crisis, fifty years ago. But this time around, it is not only the economy's performance that is called into question, but also the State's. The very public sector that was instrumental to the previous solution is now part of the new crisis. (Carnoy, 1984, 246)

Marxists are not alone in their pessimism. Poggi (1978, 145–146), for example, enumerates six problems he considers widespread throughout Western states and descriptive, as well, of most, if not all, others. They can be summarized as follows:

1.   Political dissent that may be subversive, on the one hand, and, on the other, repressed in unconstitutional ways.
2.   The inability of welfare systems to remedy inequities at the same time as they become fiscally overwhelming.
3.   Failures of political leadership, including leaders behaving in ways that call into question the moral foundations of the society.
4.   The inability of legal machinery to adequately protect the innocent while it punishes offenders, regardless of their status.
5.   Growing bureaucracies alongside growing ineffectiveness.
6.   Failure to steer the economy along a path of stable growth.

Such assessments of political states suggest that state-centered analyses may take over from economics the title of "dismal science."

Pessimistic assessments of state and society have often preceded analyses of revolution and the pressure for major social changes. It is no exaggeration to say that societal problems and their relation to social and political revolution were the stimulus to the founding of modern sociology. From Comte to Spencer, Marx, Durkheim, and Weber, understanding the sources of revolutions, accounting for their effects, and predicting their occurrence were the rationale for the discipline of sociology (or Marx's alternative). To the extent that we continue to be concerned with finding ways in which knowledge can be applied to the creation of a better society, there has to be dismay at the continuing existence of intractable inequities and terrifying conflicts. For the most part, the roots of revolution have been sought in oppression and associated grievances (e.g., Gurr, 1970), in an imbalance in values resulting from rapid or uneven social change (e.g., Smelser, 1963), or in the availability of resources for those already organized (e.g., Tilly, 1975). In contrast, Skocpol (1979, 24–33) has been in the forefront of those who take the state seriously as the primary actor in revolutionary situations. She concludes her analysis of revolutions in France, Russia, and China with the following statement:

Both the occurrence of the revolutionary situations in the first place and the nature of the New Regimes that emerged from the revolutionary conflicts depended fundamentally upon the structures of state organizations and their partially autonomous and dynamic relationships to domestic class and political forces, as well as their positions in relation to other states abroad. (Skocpol, 1979, 284)

When we come to examine the results of revolution itself, it is disappointing that it never seems to produce the ideal society or state (Arendt, 1965, 220). Again and again, the aftermath of political revolution has either perpetuated old cleavages and inequities or replaced them with new ones (see Goldstone, 1986, 207–317 and the examples that he includes).

Public Policy

In efforts to bring about change, the state can be viewed as an adversary, either because of its passive support for dominant social and economic interests or because of its actively coercive actions. It can also be viewed as a more benign actor whose policy-directed activities affect all those who come under its control. Policymaking, to be sure, involves not only legislative efforts at producing change but also, and probably more frequently, creation of laws and associated agencies for buttressing existing distributions of power. But whatever the desired outcome, the sociologist ignores an important component of state activity if its policymaking role is ignored.

In the study of policymaking, the big issues today are accounting for how policies come into being and are implemented. Kingdon (1980), a political scientist, proposes looking at policymaking as a process divisible into four stages. The first relates to setting the agenda, in which issues become politically salient. The second stage occurs when there is specification of alternatives from which policy choices can be made. These are followed by authoritative decisions, that is, ones that will be binding on the collectivity. Finally, the process needs to take into account the implementation of decisions. Applied to his analysis of national health and transportation issues, Kingdon pays most attention to the first two stages—agenda setting and factors affecting alternatives from which choices are selected. Agenda setting is primarily the result of interests mobilized, both inside and outside government. Within the U.S. federal government, career civil servants have little impact on agenda setting, more on alternatives, and most on implementation. This contrasts with Heclo's (1974) analysis of income maintenance policies in Britain and Sweden, where civil servants played an important role in designing alternatives.

In a major sociological effort to examine the role of the state in policymaking, Laumann and Knoke (1987) see influence taking place through large formal organizations, including organizations of participants who are not an intrinsic part of government. Using energy and health issues as their context, they find participants linked through information, with everyone wanting information that is timely and trustworthy. Participants are activated through communication networks that enable them to mobilize resources for affecting authorities.

In a third approach to policymaking, emphasis is on state structural charac-teristics, like degree of bureaucratization and openness to experts, as well as on the programs of political parties. In this way Weir and Skocpol (1985) try to account for why, in response to the Great Depression of the 1930s, the BLP sought remedies in social insurance, and the Swedish Social Democrats, in public works.

While Laumann and Knoke give most attention to the organizational bases of the participants, Kingdon to the formal structures of government, and Weir and Skocpol to differences between political parties, they are similar in specifying the interests involved and uncovering those actors whose mobilization has an impact on the outcome. They differ considerably, however, in the actors they include and the weight they assign to historical versus contemporary factors.

If the state means more than the national government and the arena in which it interacts with other collective actors, then room is left for the policy orientations of local governments. One possibility, illustrated by James's (1988) study of voter registration, indicates how conflicts between national and local states are mani-fested.

The importance of local conditions is demonstrated by Clark and Ferguson's (1983) research on responses by 62 cities to ''fiscal strain''—government spending commitments that exceeded resources. The authors examine responses in terms of the political cultures of cities, based on characteristics like partisan composition, citizen preferences, style of politics, and types of groups politically active. They conclude, for example, that Democratic cities and ones with an ethnic, in-group culture do well in meeting fiscal crises where they rely on low-visibility sources of revenue (Clark and Ferguson, 1983, 247–248).

Friedland and Palmer (1984) contrast state power at the local level with the power of business as manifested in ''the capacity to acquire desired public policy outcomes'' (Friedland and Palmer, 1984, 394). Based on a review of the literature, they conclude that businesses will participate more in local policymaking where they are economically dominant and dependent on local conditions for growth.

When attention is shifted from the process or content of policymaking to the outcome of particular cases—for example, the ''war on poverty'' or efforts to bring about equal employment opportunities for blacks and women—then we often seem to be in much the same place as the students of revolution. That is, either we are stuck in a morass of detail or we are dissatisfied with the results of legislative interventions. So Burstein (1985, 155–177), in considering the future of equal employment opportunity, asks why it has taken so long for blacks and women to catch up with white men. Needless to say, he has no simple answers; factors of prejudice, education, economy, and politics are reviewed, of which only the last relates to legislative efforts. Another example that focuses on unintended outcomes is found in William J. Wilson's (1987, 110–118) review of policy measures de-signed to help poor blacks; they have been most beneficial to those blacks already in a more advantaged position.

Such dissatisfaction with policy outcomes has generated a whole body of literature, especially in political science. For example, in one of the most widely cited works in the field, partially subtitled "How Great Expectations in Washington Are Dashed in Oakland; Or, Why It's Amazing That Federal Programs Work at All," Pressman and Wildavsky (1979) attribute failure to the process by which good laws are implemented. They differentiate between policies that try to change government (relatively easy to accomplish) and those directed to changing the public (almost impossible).

THE STATE AND EVERYDAY LIFE

Dissatisfaction with policy outcomes is virtually endemic, like the evaluations made of revolutions. This response should neither be ignored nor attributed, as Wildavsky first suggests, to problems of implementation. Sociological concern with the state is premised on the ability of the state, through its organizations and participants, to act in ways that have consequences for the society. But if consequences are almost always different from what is intended, once they move beyond narrow, operational spheres of government, we are left to wonder at the utility of current state/society and public/private distinctions. That is, unless we wish to attribute unexpected and undesirable outcomes to either sheer incompetence or malicious intent, we have to consider why the state, operating autonomously, still cannot create the conditions for accomplishing desired results. Let us try to penetrate these issues by returning to the experiences of identifiable individuals.

Not every class of students I teach is as perceptive as the one I introduced at the outset of this volume in commenting on the meaning of politics. In another class, at the end of a quarter of reading and discussion on some of the same topics, one student told me that, while the class had been interesting enough, he did not expect that it would have any relevance to his future career in sales. He lacked the foresight to see how the organization of his work world would involve the exercise of power; how disputes could arise over the legitimacy of rules, directives, and managers; how his rewards would be affected by his contribution to the goals of his company as well as his efforts; or how he would be constrained by rules and directives, whether or not he had a part in their formulation. Nor had he been aware of how his experiences in the university could be viewed as political ones, in ways that students outlined in Chapter 1.

Perhaps most surprising was this student's insensitivity to the impact of the state. As a student, he was affected by the state legislature's vote for the university's budget and the subsequent actions of the board of trustees in setting tuition fees. As a male, he was bound by the requirements to register for the draft, an activity that had been at the center of student protest during the Vietnam war. As a resident of the United States, he must pay taxes and abide by its laws, and, as a citizen, he is empowered to vote and to travel abroad under the state's protection. Yet none of these things came consciously to mind as a reason for wanting to understand politics. It is as though he took all these rights and responsibilities for granted as part of life in the United States.

My unfortunate student's desire to be happily ignorant of how he participates in the political world cannot be defended, but it does deserve to be evaluated. This evaluation needs to be made in light of Poggi's (1978, 137–138) argument that the state is increasing its encroachment on the life of its citizens, thereby blurring distinctions between public and private domains. As a consequence, distinctions between state and society are also blurred. To my student, at least, there was no difference.

What began in this chapter as a plea for greater sociological awareness of the independent effects of the state is now situated in the context of ever more inclusive definitions of the state. For example, Skocpol suggests that we approach the state as a cultural configuration:

> States matter not simply because of the goal-oriented activities of state officials. They matter because their organizational configurations, along with their overall patterns of activity, affect political culture, encourage some kinds of group formation and collective political actions (but not others), and make possible the raising of certain political issues (but not others). (Skocpol, 1985, 21)

Similarly, Thomas and Meyer (1984, 478) want us to focus on the state "as an institution or as an entity essentially cultural in character." If we follow these suggestions, what will be the outcome? Will it be a way of further blurring the lines between state and society because it moves the impact of the state out of the realm of deliberate action and into that of social structure and culture? Or will it be a means of relegating the state to a distinct and narrow arena of activity by equating it with political institutions—those norms, values, and statuses concerned with maintaining social control over a given territory? In either case, it could leave the autonomous state as an abstraction without much explanatory power.

If my student could take for granted the political context of life in the United States, we cannot. Nor should we retreat from efforts to account for state actions or for the consequences of existing political structures. None of these activities is likely to make us "political sociologists." Professor Sartori notwithstanding, there is a need for a sociology of politics, one that explains the sources of continuity and change in the nature of society, and not just in the nature of the state.

NOTE

1. This volume's emphasis on internal political problems leads to the unavoidable omission of problems arising from relations among political units and hence to a failure to evaluate works that emphasize those relations, like Wallerstein's (1974; 1980) world system approach.

REFERENCES

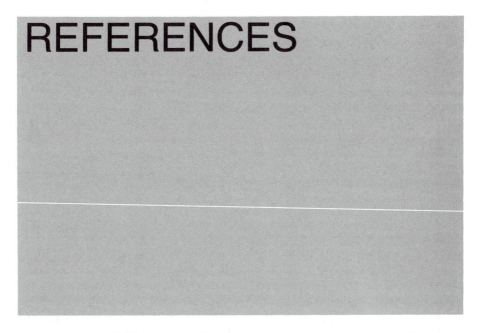

Abel, Theodore. (1966) *The Nazi Movement: Why Hitler Came to Power*. New York: Atherton.

Albornoz, Orlando. (1966) "Academic Freedom and Higher Education in Latin America." A special issue of *Comparative Education Review* 10 (June). Pp. 250–256 in S. M. Lipset, ed., *Student Politics*. Berkeley: Institute of International Studies, University of California.

Alford, Robert R. (1975) *Health Care Politics: Ideological and Interest Group Barriers to Reform*. Chicago: University of Chicago Press.

Alford, Robert R., and Roger F. Friedland. (1975) "Political Participation and Public Policy." *Annual Review of Sociology* 1: 429–479.

———. (1985) *Powers of Theory: Capitalism, the State, and Democracy*. Cambridge, England: Cambridge University Press.

Allison, Graham. (1971) *Essence of Decision: Explaining the Cuban Missile Crisis*. Boston: Little Brown.

Almond, Gabriel A., and Sidney Verba. (1963) *The Civic Culture: Public Attitudes and Democracy in Five Nations*. Princeton, NJ: Princeton University Press.

Althusser, Louis. (1969) *For Marx*. New York: Pantheon.

Andersen, Kristi. (1979) *Creation of a Democratic Majority, 1928–1936*. Chicago: University of Chicago Press.

Anderson, Perry. (1974) *Lineages of the Absolutist State*. London: New Left.

Arendt, Hannah. (1965) *On Revolution*. New York: Viking.

Aristotle. (1962) *The Politics*. Baltimore: Penguin.

Avineri, Shlomo. (1968) *The Social and Political Thought of Karl Marx*. Cambridge, England: Cambridge University Press.

Badie, Bertrand, and Pierre Birnbaum. (1983) *The Sociology of the State*, trans. Arthur Goldhammer. Chicago: University of Chicago Press.

Banfield, Edward C. (1961) *Political Influence*. New York: Free Press.

Barnes, Samuel H., Max Kaase, et al. (1979) *Political Action: Mass Participation in Five Western Democracies*. Beverly Hills, CA: Sage.

Bassett, Keith. (1984) "Labour, Socialism, and Local Democracy." Pp. 82–108 in M. Boddy and C. Fudge, eds., *Local Socialism?* London: Macmillan.

Beatty, Jack. (1983) "The Vanishing Voter." *The New Republic* (March 21), 35–37.

Bell, Daniel. (1962) *The End of Ideology*, rev. ed. New York: Collier.

Bendix, Reinhard et al., eds. (1964) *Nation-Building and Citizenship*. New York: Wiley.

––––––. (1968) "Introduction." Pp. 2–13 in Bendix et al., eds., *State and Society*. Berkeley: University of California Press.

––––––. (1978) *Kings or People: Power and the Mandate to Rule*. Berkeley: University of California Press.

Berelson, Bernard, Paul F. Lazarsfeld, and William N. McPhee. (1954) *Voting: A Study of Opinion Formation in a Presidential Campaign*. Chicago: University of Chicago Press.

Bernard, Jean-Paul. (1971) *Les Rouges: Libéralisme, nationalisme et anticléricalisme au milieu du XIXe siècle*. Montréal: Les presses de l'université du Québec.

Birch, A. (1959) *Small Town Politics*. London: Oxford University Press.

Brown, Courtney. (1987) "Voter Mobilization and Party Competition in a Volatile Electorate." *American Sociological Review* 52 (February), 59–72.

Burke, Edmund. (1968) *Reflections on the Revolution in France and on the Proceedings in Certain Societies in London Relative to That Event*, ed. Conor Cruise O'Brien. Baltimore: Penguin.

Burnham, Walter Dean. (1983) *The Current Crisis in American Politics*. New York: Oxford University Press.

Burstein, Paul. (1985) *Discrimination, Jobs, and Politics*. Chicago: University of Chicago Press.

Butler, David, and Donald Stokes. (1969) *Political Change in Britain*. New York: St. Martin's.

Cancian, Francesca M. (1985) "Gender Politics: Love and Power in the Private and Public Spheres." Pp. 253–264 in Alice S. Rossi, ed., *Gender and the Life Course*. New York: Aldine.

Cantril, Hadley. (1941) *The Psychology of Social Movements*. New York: Wiley.

Carnoy, Martin. (1984) *The State and Political Theory*. Princeton, NJ: Princeton University Press.

Carter, Jimmy. (1976) Interview. *Playboy Magazine* 83 (November), 63–86.

Carter, Paul A. (1956) *The Decline and Revival of the Social Gospel*. Ithaca, NY: Cornell University Press.

Castells, Manuel. (1977) *The Urban Question: A Marxist Approach,* trans. Alan Sheridan. Cambridge, MA: MIT Press.

Cawson, A., and P. Saunders. (1983) "Corporatism, Competitive Politics and Class Struggle." Pp. 8–27 in Roger King, ed., *Capital and Politics*. London: Routledge and Kegan Paul.

Clark, Terry Nichols, and Lorna Crowley Ferguson. (1983) *City Money: Political Processes, Fiscal Strain, and Retrenchment*. New York: Columbia University Press.

Clarke, Harold D., Jane Jenson, Lawrence LeDuc, and Jon H. Pammett. (1979) *Political Choice in Canada*. Toronto: McGraw-Hill Ryerson.

Cole, G. D. H. (1937) "Fabianism." *Encyclopedia of the Social Sciences*, vol. 6. New York: Macmillan.

Coleman, James S. (1974) *Power and the Structure of Society*. New York: Norton.

Collins, Randall. (1968) "A Comparative Approach to Political Sociology." Pp. 42–67 in Reinhard Bendix et al., eds., *State and Society*. Berkeley: University of California Press.

————. (1982) *Sociological Insight*. New York: Oxford University Press.

Converse, Philip E. (1964) "The Nature of Belief Systems in Mass Publics." Pp. 206–261 in David E. Apter, ed., *Ideology and Discontent*. New York: Free Press.

Converse, Philip E., Angus Campbell, Warren E. Miller, and Donald E. Stokes. (1961) "Stability and Change in 1960: A Reinstating Election." *American Political Science Review* 55 (June), 269–280.

Cotter, Cornelius P., James L. Gibson, John F. Bibby, and Robert J. Huckshorn. (1984) *Party Organizations in American Politics*. New York: Praeger.

Crozier, Michel. (1964) *The Bureaucratic Phenomenon*. Chicago: University of Chicago Press.

Cyert, Richard M., and James G. March. (1963) *A Behavioral Theory of the Firm*. Englewood Cliffs, NJ: Prentice Hall.

Dahl, Robert A. (1961) *Who Governs?* New Haven, CT: Yale University Press.

————. (1971) *Polyarchy: Participation and Opposition*. New Haven, CT: Yale University Press.

Dearlove, J. (1973) *The Politics of Policy in Local Government*. London: Cambridge University Press.

————. (1979). *The Re-organisation of British Local Government*. London: Cambridge University Press.

Derthick, Martha. (1979) *Policymaking for Social Security*. Washington, DC: Brookings Institute.

Deutsch, Karl W. (1966) *Nationalism and Social Communication: An Inquiry into the Foundations of Nationality*. Cambridge, MA: MIT Press.

DeWaal, Frans. (1982) *Chimpanzee Politics*. New York: Harper & Row.

Dunleavy, P. (1981) *The Politics of Mass Housing in Britain*. Oxford: Clarendon.

Duverger, Maurice. (1963) *Political Parties: Their Organization and Activity in the Modern State*, trans. Barbara and Robert North. New York: Wiley.

Elcock, Howard James. (1982) *Local Government, Politicians, Professionals, and the Public in Local Authorities*. London: Methuen.

Emerson, Richard M. (1962) "Power-Dependence Relations." *American Sociological Review* 27 (February), 31–40.

Emerson, Rupert. (1960) *From Empire to Nation: The Rise to Self-Assertion of Asian and African Peoples*. Cambridge, MA: Harvard University Press.

Engelmann, F. C., and Mildred A. Schwartz. (1981) "Perceptions of Austrian Federalism." *Publius* 11 (Winter), 81–93.

Epstein, Leon. (1980) *Political Parties in Western Democracies*, new ed. New Brunswick, NJ: Transaction.

————. (1986) *Political Parties in the American Mold*. Madison: University of Wisconsin Press.

Feld, Scott L., and Bernard Grofman. (1988) "Ideological Consistency as a Collective Phenomenon." *American Political Science Review* 82 (September), 773–788.

Flacks, Richard. (1971) *Youth and Social Change*. Chicago: Markham.

Frank, Andre Gunder. (1967) *Capitalism and Underdevelopment in Latin America*. New York: Monthly Review.

Frankovic, Kathleen. (1982) "Sex and Politics: New Alignments, Old Issues." *PS* 15 (Summer), 439–448.

Freeman, Jo. (1975) *The Women's Liberation Movement*. New York: McKay.

Free Speech Movement. (1965) "The FSM Speaks." Pp. 201–219 in S. M. Lipset and S. S.

Wolin, eds., *The Berkeley Student Revolt: Facts and Interpretations*. Garden City, NY: Doubleday Anchor.

Friedland, Roger, and Donald Palmer. (1984) "Park Place and Main Street: Business and the Urban Power Structure." *American Review of Sociology* 10, 393–416.

Frost, Peter J. et al. (1985) *Organizational Culture*. Beverly Hills, CA: Sage.

Gallie, Duncan. (1983) *Social Inequality and Class Radicalism in France and Britain*. Cambridge, England: Cambridge University Press.

Gamson, William A. (1968) *Power and Discontent*. Homewood, IL: Dorsey.

Geertz, Clifford. (1973) *The Interpretation of Cultures*. New York: Basic.

Gitlin, Todd. (1987) *The Sixties: Years of Hope, Days of Rage*. New York: Bantam.

Glazer, Nathan, and Daniel P. Moynihan. (1970) *Beyond the Melting Pot: Negroes, Puerto Ricans, Jews, Italians, and Irish of New York City*, 2nd ed. Cambridge, MA: MIT Press.

Goldstone, Jack A., ed. (1986) *Revolutions: Theoretical, Comparative, and Historical Studies*. Orlando, FL: Harcourt Brace Jovanovich.

Goody, Jack, ed. (1968) *Literacy in Traditional Societies*. Cambridge, England: Cambridge University Press.

Gosnell, Howard. (1935) *Negro Politicians*. Chicago: University of Chicago Press.

———. (1968) *Machine Politics: Chicago Model*, 2nd ed. Chicago: University of Chicago Press.

Gouldner, Alvin W. (1954) *Patterns of Industrial Democracy*. Glencoe, IL: Free Press.

Graff, Harvey J. (1986) *The Legacies of Literacy: Continuities and Contradictions in Western Culture and Society*. Bloomington, IN: University of Indiana Press.

Gray, John. (1986) *Liberalism*. Minneapolis: University of Minnesota Press.

Greenstone, J. David. (1969) *Labor in American Politics*. New York: Random House Vintage.

Grimes, Alan P. (1967) *The Puritan Ethic and Woman Suffrage*. New York: Oxford University Press.

Gurr, T. R. (1970) *Why Men Rebel*. Princeton, NJ: Princeton University Press.

Guterbock, Thomas M. (1980) *Machine Politics in Transition*. Chicago: University of Chicago Press.

Habermas, Jurgen. (1975) *Legitimation Crisis*, trans. Thomas McCarthy. Boston: Beacon.

Hamilton, Richard F. (1982) *Who Voted for Hitler?* Princeton, NJ: Princeton University Press.

Hamilton, Richard F., and James D. Wright. (1986) *The State of the Masses*. New York: Aldine.

Hartz, Louis. (1955) *The Liberal Tradition in America*. New York: Harcourt Brace.

———. (1964) *The Founding of New Societies*. New York: Harcourt, Brace, and World.

Hawley, Amos. (1963) "Community Power and Urban Renewal Success." *American Journal of Sociology* 68 (January), 422–431.

Hawley, Willis D., and Frederick M. Wirt, eds. (1968) *The Search for Community Power*. Englewood Cliffs, NJ: Prentice Hall.

Heberle, Rudolf. (1951) *Social Movements*. New York: Appleton-Century-Crofts.

Heclo, Hugh. (1974) *Modern Social Politics in Britain and Sweden*. New Haven, CT: Yale University Press.

Heirich, Max, and Sam Kaplan. (1965) "Yesterday's Discord." Pp. 10–35 in S. M. Lipset and S. S. Wolin, eds., *The Berkeley Student Revolt: Facts and Interpretations*. Garden City, NY: Doubleday Anchor.

Hicks, John R. (1961) *The Populist Revolt*. Lincoln: University of Nebraska Press.

Hill, B. W. (1976) *The Growth of Parliamentary Parties, 1689–1742.* London: Allen and Unwin.

Hobhouse, L. T. (1911) *Liberalism.* New York: Holt.

Horowitz, Gad. (1968) *Canadian Labour in Politics.* Toronto: University of Toronto Press.

Horowitz, Irving Louis. (1966) *Three Worlds of Development.* New York: Oxford University Press.

Howard, Dick. (1977) *The Marxian Legacy.* New York: Urizen.

Hunter, Floyd. (1963) *Community Power Structure.* New York: Doubleday.

Huntington, Samuel P. (1968) *Political Order in Changing Societies.* New Haven, CT: Yale University Press.

Inkeles, Alex, and David H. Smith. (1974) *Becoming Modern: Individual Change in Six Developing Countries.* Cambridge, MA: Harvard University Press.

Irving, John. (1959) *The Social Credit Movement in Alberta.* Toronto: University of Toronto Press.

Iyengar, Shanto, and Donald R. Kinder. (1987) *News That Matters.* Chicago: University of Chicago Press.

Jackman, Robert W. (1975) *Politics and Social Equality: A Comparative Analysis.* New York: Wiley.

James, David R. (1988) "The Transformation of the Southern Racial State: Class and Race Determinants of Local-State Structures." *American Sociological Review* 53 (April), 191–208.

Jenkins, Craig. (1983) "Resource Mobilization Theory and the Study of Mobilization." *Annual Review of Sociology* 9, 527–553.

Jennings, M. K., and Richard G. Niemi. (1981) *Generations and Politics.* Princeton, NJ: Princeton University Press.

Jensen, Richard. (1971) *The Winning of the Midwest.* Chicago: University of Chicago Press.

Jessop, Bob. (1982) *The Capitalist State: Marxist Theories and Methods.* New York: New York University Press.

Jones, G. (1969) *Borough Politics.* London: Macmillan.

Kay, Geoffrey. (1975) *Development and Underdevelopment: A Marxist Analysis.* London: Macmillan.

Keeter, Scott. (1985) "Public Opinion in 1984." Pp. 91–111 in Gerald Pomper et al., *The Election of 1984.* Chatham, NJ: Chatham House.

Kelley, Jonathan, and Herbert S. Klein. (1986) "Revolution and the Rebirth of Inequality: Stratification in Post-Revolutionary Society." Pp. 209–218 in Jack A. Goldstone, ed., *Revolutions: Theoretical, Comparative, and Historical Studies.* Orlando, FL: Harcourt Brace Jovanovich.

Kelley, Stanley, Jr., Richard E. Ayres, and William G. Bowen. (1967) "Registration and Voting: Putting First Things First." *American Political Science Review* 61 (June), 359–379.

Keniston, Kenneth. (1965) *The Uncommitted: Alienated Youth in American Society.* New York: Harcourt, Brace, and World.

Key, V. O., Jr. (1949) *Southern Politics in State and Nation.* New York: Knopf.

———. (1955) "A Theory of Critical Elections." *Journal of Politics* 17, 3–18.

———. (1959) "Secular Realignment and the Party System." *Journal of Politics* 21, 198–210.

Killian, Lewis. (1975) *The Impossible Revolution, Phase 2: Black Power and the American Dream.* New York: Random House.

Kinder, Donald R. (1983) "Diversity and Complexity in American Public Opinion." Pp. 389–425 in Ada W. Finifter, ed., *Political Science: The State of the Discipline*. Washington, DC: American Political Science Association.

Kinder, Donald R., and David O. Sears. (1985) "Public Opinion and Political Action." Pp. 659–741 in Gardner Lindzey and Elliot Aronson, eds., *The Handbook of Social Psychology*, Vol. II, 3rd ed. New York: Random House.

King, Roger. (1986) *The State in Modern Society: New Directions in Political Sociology*. Chatham, NJ: Chatham House.

Kingdon, John W. (1980) *Agendas, Alternatives, and Public Policies*. Boston: Little Brown.

Klein, Ethel. (1984) *Gender Politics*. Cambridge, MA: Harvard University Press.

Kornhauser, William. (1959) *The Politics of Mass Society*. Glencoe, IL: Free Press.

Krasner, Stephen D. (1978) "United States Commercial and Monetary Policy: Unravelling the Paradox of External Strength and Internal Weakness." Pp. 51–87 in Peter J. Katzenstein, ed., *Between Power and Plenty*. Madison, WI: University of Wisconsin Press.

Kuczynski, Jurgen. (1967) *The Rise of the Working Class*, trans. C. T. A. Ray. New York: McGraw-Hill.

Laitin, David D. (1985) "Hegemony and Religious Conflict: British Imperial Control and Political Cleavages in Yorubaland." Pp. 285–316 in Peter Evans et al., eds. *Bringing the State Back In*. Cambridge, England: Cambridge University Press.

Lamis, Alexander P. (1984) *The Two-Party South*. New York: Oxford University Press.

Lane, Robert E. (1959) *Political Life: Why People Get Involved in Politics*. New York: Free Press.

———. (1962) *Political Ideology: Why the American Common Man Believes What He Does*. New York: Free Press.

Lang, Kurt, and Gladys Engel Lang. (1983) *The Battle for Public Opinion*. New York: Columbia University Press.

Lasswell, Harold. (1958) *Politics: Who Gets What, When, How*. Cleveland: World.

Laumann, Edward O., and David Knoke. (1987) *The Organizational State: Social Choice in National Policy Domains*. Madison: University of Wisconsin Press.

Lazarsfeld, Paul F., Bernard Berelson, and Hazel Gaudet. (1944) *The People's Choice*. New York: Columbia University Press.

Lenin, V. I. (1943) *What Is to Be Done?* New York: International.

Levine, David O. (1986) *The American College and the Culture of Aspiration, 1915–1940*. Ithaca, NY: Cornell University Press.

Lipset, S. M. (1963) *The First New Nation*. New York: Basic.

———. (1968) *Agrarian Socialism: The Cooperative Commonwealth Federation in Saskatchewan*, updated. Garden City, NY: Doubleday Anchor.

———.(1976) *Rebellion in the University*. Chicago: University of Chicago.

———. (1977) "Why No Socialism in the United States?" Pp. 31–149 in Seweryn Bialer and Sophia Sluzar, eds., *Sources of Contemporary Radicalism*. New York: Westview.

———. (1981) *Political Man: The Social Bases of Politics*, expanded and updated. Baltimore: Johns Hopkins University Press.

———. (1985) "The Elections, the Economy and Public Opinion, 1984." *PS* (Winter), 28–38.

Lipset, S. M., and Earl Raab. (1978) *The Politics of Unreason*, 2nd ed. Chicago: University of Chicago Press.

Lipset, S. M., and Stein Rokkan. (1967) "Cleavage Structures, Party Systems, and Voter

Alignments: An Introduction." Pp. 1–64 in Lipset and Rokkan, eds., *Party Systems and Voter Alignments*. New York: Free Press.

Lipset, S. M., and William Schneider. (1983) *The Confidence Gap: Business, Labor, and Government in the Public Mind*. New York: Free Press.

Locke, John. (1966) *The Second Treatise of Government*, ed. J. W. Gough, 3rd ed. Oxford: Blackwell.

Lorwin, Val R. (1966) "Belgium: Religion, Class, and Language in National Politics." Pp. 147–187 in Robert A. Dahl, ed., *Political Oppositions in Western Democracies*. New Haven, CT: Yale University Press.

Lugard, Frederick. (1922) *The Dual Mandate in British Tropical Africa*. London: Frank Cass.

Macpherson, C. B. (1962) *Democracy in Alberta: Social Credit and the Party System*, 2nd ed. Toronto: University of Toronto Press.

Maier, Charles. (1976) "Some Recent Studies in Fascism." *Journal of Modern History* 48 (September), 506–521.

Markoff, John. (1986) "Literacy and Revolt: Some Empirical Notes on 1789 in France." *American Journal of Sociology* 92 (September), 323–349.

Marshall, T. H. (1964) *Class, Citizenship, and Social Development*. Garden City, NY: Doubleday Anchor.

Martin, John Frederick. (1979) *Civil Rights and the Crisis of Liberalism: The Democratic Party, 1945–1976*. Boulder, CO: Westview.

Marx, Karl. (1971) *The Grundrisse*, ed. and trans. David McLellan. New York: Harper.

Marx, Karl, and Friedrich Engels. (1959) *Basic Writings on Politics and Philosophy*, ed. Lewis S. Feuer. Garden City, NY: Doubleday Anchor.

Matthews, Donald R., and James W. Prothro. (1966) *Negroes and the New Southern Politics*. New York: Harcourt, Brace, and World.

Mayhew, David R. (1986) *Placing Parties in American Politics*. Princeton, NJ: Princeton University Press.

McCarthy, John D., and Meyer N. Zald. (1973) *The Trend of Social Movements in America: Professionalization and Resource Mobilization*. Morristown, NJ: General Learning.

McKenzie, Robert. (1964) *British Political Parties*, 2nd ed. New York: Praeger.

McKenzie, Robert, and Allan Silver. (1968) *Angels in Marble*. Chicago: University of Chicago Press.

Merton, Robert K. (1957) *Social Theory and Social Structure*, rev. and enlarged. Glencoe, IL: Free Press.

Michels, Robert. (1962) *Political Parties: A Sociological Study of the Oligarchical Tendencies of Modern Democracy*, trans. Eden and Cedar Paul. New York: Collier.

Miliband, Ralph. (1977) *Marxism and Politics*. Oxford, England: Oxford University Press.

Mill, John Stuart. (1965) *Principles of Political Economy*, ed. W. J. Ashley. New York: Kelley.

Mills, C. Wright. (1956) *The Power Elite*. New York: Oxford University Press.

Moore, Barrington, Jr. (1966) *Social Origins of Dictatorship and Democracy: Lord and Peasant in the Making of the Modern World*. Boston: Beacon.

Neuman, W. Russell. (1986) *The Paradox of Mass Politics*. Cambridge, MA: Harvard University Press.

Neumann, Sigmund. (1956) "Toward a Comparative Study of Political Parties." Pp. 395–421 in S. Neumann, ed., *Modern Political Parties*. Chicago: University of Chicago Press.

Nie, Norman, Sidney Verba, and John Petrocik. (1976) *The Changing American Voter.* Cambridge, MA: Harvard University Press.

———. (1979) *The Changing American Voter,* enlarged. Cambridge, MA: Harvard University Press.

———. (1981) Reply. *American Political Science Review* 75 (March), 149–152.

Niemi, Richard G., and Herbert F. Weisberg. (1984) *Controversies in Voting Behavior,* 2nd ed. Washington, DC: Congressional Quarterly.

Nisbet, Robert. (1986) *Conservatism.* Minneapolis: University of Minnesota Press.

Noelle-Neumann, Elisabeth. (1984) *The Spiral of Silence: Public Opinion, Our Social Skin.* Chicago: University of Chicago Press.

Oberschall, Anthony. (1973) *Social Conflict and Social Movements.* Englewood Cliffs, NJ: Prentice Hall.

Oglesby, Carl. (1971) "Trapped in a System." Pp. 17–26 in Matthew F. Stolz, ed., *Politics of the New Left.* Beverly Hills, CA: Glencoe.

Olson, Keith W. (1974) *The G.I. Bill, the Veterans, and the Colleges.* Lexington: University of Kentucky Press.

Olson, Mancur. (1971) *The Logic of Collective Action.* Cambridge, MA: Harvard University Press.

———. (1982) *Rise and Decline of Nations: Economic Growth, Stagflation, and Social Rigidities.* New Haven, CT: Yale University Press.

O'Neill, William L. (1969) *The Woman Movement: Feminism in the United States and England.* Chicago: Quadrangle.

Orum, Anthony. (1989) *Introduction to Political Sociology,* 3rd ed. Englewood Cliffs, NJ: Prentice Hall.

Oxaal, Ivar. (1968) *Black Intellectuals Come to Power.* Cambridge, MA: Shenkman.

Paige, Jeffery M. (1975) *Agrarian Revolution: Social Movements and Export Agriculture in the Underdeveloped World.* New York: Free Press.

Parsons, Talcott. (1960) *Structure and Process in Modern Societies.* Glencoe, IL: Free Press.

———. (1966) *Societies: Evolutionary and Comparative Perspectives.* Englewood Cliffs, NJ: Prentice Hall.

———. (1971) *The System of Modern Societies.* Englewood Cliffs, NJ: Prentice Hall.

Penner, Norman. (1977) *The Canadian Left.* Scarborough, Ont.: Prentice Hall of Canada.

Perman, Michael. (1987) *Emancipation and Reconstruction, 1862–1879.* Arlington Heights, IL: Harlan Davidson.

Peterson, Paul E. (1981) *City Limits.* Chicago: University of Chicago Press.

Pfeffer, Jeffrey, and Gerald R. Salancik. (1978) *The External Control of Organizations.* New York: Harper & Row.

Piven, Frances Fox. (1985) "Women and State: Ideology, Power, and the Welfare State." Pp. 265–287 in Alice S. Rossi, *Gender and the Life Course.* New York: Aldine.

Piven, Frances Fox, and Richard A. Cloward. (1971) *Regulating the Poor.* New York: Random House.

Poggi, Gianfranco. (1978) *The Development of the Modern State.* Stanford, CA: Stanford University Press.

Pomper, Gerald M. (1975) *Voters' Choice: Varieties of American Electoral Behavior.* New York: Dodd, Mead.

———. (1985) "The Nominations." Pp. 1–34 in Pomper et al., *The Election of 1984.* Chatham, NJ: Chatham House.

Poole, Keith T., and L. Harmon Ziegler. (1985) *Women, Public Opinion, and Politics.* New York: Longman.

Pressman, Jeffrey, and Aaron Wildavsky. (1979) *Implementation,* 2nd ed. Berkeley: University of California Press.

Przeworski, Adam. (1985) *Capitalism and Social Democracy.* Cambridge, England: Cambridge University Press.

Randall, Vicky. (1987) *Women and Politics: An International Perspective,* 2nd ed. Chicago: University of Chicago Press.

Roberts, Donald F., and Nathan Maccoby. (1985) "Effects of Mass Communication." Pp. 539–598 in Gardner Lindzey and Elliot Aronson, eds., *The Handbook of Social Psychology II,* 3rd ed. New York: Random House.

Roethlisberger, F. J., and William J. Dickson. (1939) *Management and the Worker.* Cambridge, MA: Harvard University Press.

Rogin, Michael P. (1967) *The Intellectuals and McCarthy: The Radical Specter.* Cambridge, MA: MIT Press.

Rose, Richard. (1971) *Governing Without Consensus: An Irish Perspective.* Boston: Beacon.

———. (1980) *Politics in England,* 3rd ed. Boston: Little, Brown.

Rosen, George. (1980) *Decision-Making Chicago-Style: The Genesis of a University of Illinois Campus.* Urbana: University of Illinois Press.

Rossiter, Clinton. (1962) *Conservatism in America,* 2nd ed. New York: Vintage.

Rover, Constance. (1967) *Women's Suffrage and Party Politics in Britain, 1866–1914.* Toronto: University of Toronto Press.

Roy, William G. (1984) "Class Conflict and Social Change in Historical Perspective." *American Review of Sociology* 10, 483–506.

Rude, G. (1980) *Ideology and Popular Protest.* New York: Pantheon.

Sartori, Giovanni. (1969) "From the Sociology of Politics to Political Sociology." Pp. 65–100 in S. M. Lipset, ed., *Politics and the Social Sciences.* New York: Oxford University Press.

Saunders, P. (1979) *Urban Politics.* London: Hutchinson.

Schlesinger, Joseph A. (1965) "Political Party Organization." Pp. 764–801 in J. G. March, ed., *Handbook of Organizations.* Chicago: Rand McNally.

Schmitter, Philippe. (1974) "Still the Century of Corporatism?" *Review of Politics* 36 (January), 85–131.

Schneider, William. (1984) "Half a Realignment." *The New Republic* (December 3), 19–22.

Schwartz, Mildred A. (1981) "Politics and Moral Causes in Canada and the United States." Pp. 65–90 in Richard F. Tomasson, ed., *Comparative Social Research,* vol. 4. Greenwich, CT: JAI.

———. (1990) *The Party Network: The Robust Organization of Illinois Republicans.* Madison: University of Madison Press.

Scott, W. Richard. (1987) *Organizations: Rational, Natural, and Open Systems,* 2nd ed. Englewood Cliffs, NJ: Prentice Hall.

Scribner, R. W. (1986) *The German Reformation.* London: Macmillan.

Sears, David O., Richard R. Lau, Tom R. Tyler, and Harris M. Allen, Jr. (1980) "Self-Interest vs. Symbolic Politics in Policy Attitudes and Presidential Voting." *American Political Science Review* 74 (September), 670–684.

Selznick, Philip. (1949) *TVA and the Grass Roots.* Berkeley: University of California Press.

Simmel, Georg. (1950) *The Sociology of Georg Simmel,* ed. and trans. Kurt Wolff. Glencoe, IL: Free Press.

Skocpol, Theda. (1979) *States and Social Revolutions.* Cambridge, England: Cambridge University Press.

———. (1985) "Bringing the State Back In: Strategies of Analysis in Current Research." Pp. 1–37 in Peter Evans, Dietrich Rueschemeyer, and Theda Skocpol, eds., *Bringing the State Back In.* Cambridge, England: Cambridge University Press.

Smelser, Neil J. (1963) *Theory of Collective Behavior.* New York: Free Press.

Smith, Lacey Baldwin. (1953) *Tudor Prelates and Politics, 1536–1558.* Princeton, NJ: Princeton University Press.

———. (1971) *Henry VIII: The Mask of Royalty.* Boston: Houghton Mifflin.

Sombart, Werner. (1976) *Why Is There No Socialism in the United States?* trans. P. M. Hocking and C. T. Husbands. White Plains, NY: Intellectual Arts and Sciences.

Sorauf, Frank J., and Paul Allen Beck. (1988) *Political Parties in America,* 6th ed. Glenview, IL: Scott, Foresman.

Stone, Clarence N. (1980) "Systemic Power in Community Decision-Making: A Restatement of Stratification Theory." *American Political Science Review* 74 (December), 978–990.

Sundquist, James L. (1973) *Dynamics of the Party System.* Washington, DC: Brookings Institute.

Sweezy, Paul. (1972) *Modern Capitalism and Other Essays.* New York: Monthly Review.

Tambiah, S. J. (1986) *Sri Lanka: Ethnic Fratricide and the Dismantling of Democracy.* Chicago: University of Chicago Press.

Teeter, Robert M. (1984) "Who Will Lead U.S. for a Generation." *Marketing News.* Detroit: Market Opinion Research (Fall).

Thomas, George M., and John W. Meyer. (1984) "The Expansion of the State." *Annual Review of Sociology* 10: 461–482.

Thompson, E. P. (1966) *The Making of the English Working Class.* New York: Random House Vintage.

Tilly, Charles. (1975) *The Formation of National States in Western Europe.* Princeton, NJ: Princeton University Press.

———. (1978) *From Mobilization to Revolution.* Reading, MA: Addison-Wesley.

Tocqueville, Alexis de. (1945) *Democracy in America,* 2 vols. New York: Vintage.

———. (1955) *The Old Regime and the French Revolution,* trans. Stuart Gilbert. Garden City, NY: Doubleday Anchor.

Touraine, Alain. (1971) *The May Movement: Revolution and Reform,* trans. L. F. X. Mayhew. New York: Random House.

Turner, Frederick Jackson. (1947) *The Frontier in American History.* New York: Henry Holt.

Verba, Sidney, and Norman Nie. (1972) *Participation in America.* New York: Harper & Row.

Wade, Mason. (1968) *The French Canadians, 1760–1967,* vol. 1, rev. ed. Toronto: Macmillan.

Wallerstein, Immanuel. (1974) *The Modern World System,* vol. I. New York: Academic.

———. (1980) *The Modern World System,* vol. II. New York: Academic.

Wattenberg, Martin P. (1984) *The Decline of American Political Parties, 1952–1980.* Cambridge, MA: Harvard University Press.

Weber, Max. (1958) *The Protestant Ethic and the Spirit of Capitalism*, trans. Talcott Parsons. New York: Scribner's.

———. (1978) *Economy and Society*, vols. I and II, ed. Guenther Roth and Claus Wittich. Berkeley: University of California Press.

Weir, Margaret, and Theda Skocpol. (1985) "State Structures and the Possibilities for 'Keynesian' Responses to the Great Depression in Sweden, Britain, and the United States." Pp. 107–163 in Peter Evans, Dietrich Rueschemeyer, and Theda Skocpol, eds., *Bringing the State Back In*. Cambridge, England: Cambridge University Press.

Whiteley, Paul. (1983) *The Labour Party in Crisis*. London: Methuen.

Wildavsky, Aaron. (1987) "Choosing Preferences by Constructing Institutions: A Cultural Theory of Preference Formation." *American Political Science Review* 81 (March), 3–21.

Wilson, James Q. (1960) *Negro Politicians*. New York: Free Press.

Wilson, Monica. (1967) "Nyakyusa Age-Villages." Pp. 217–227 in Ronald Cohen and John Middleton, eds., *Comparative Political Systems: Studies in the Politics of Preindustrial Societies*. Garden City, NY: Natural History.

Wilson, William J. (1987) *The Truly Disadvantaged: The Inner City, the Underclass, and Public Policy*. Chicago: University of Chicago Press.

Wolfe, Alan. (1985) "The Death of Social Democracy." *The New Republic* (February 25), 21–23.

Wollstonecraft, Mary. (1982) *A Critical Edition of Mary Wollstonecraft's A Vindication of the Rights of Woman: With Strictures on Political and Moral Subjects*, ed. Ulrich H. Hardt. Troy, NY: Whitston.

Wright, James D. (1976) *The Dissent of the Governed: Alienation and Democracy in America*. New York: Academic.

Wrong, Dennis H. (1980) *Power: Its Forms, Bases and Uses*. New York: Harper & Row.

Wuthnow, Robert. (1985) "State Structures and Ideological Outcomes." *American Sociological Review* 50 (December), 799–821.

Yale Law Journal. (1954) "The American Medical Association: Power, Purpose, and Politics in Organized Medicine—The Political Basis of Power." *Yale Law Journal* 63 (May), 937–1022.

Zald, Mayer N., and Roberta Asch. (1966) "Social Movement Organizations: Growth, Decay and Change." *Social Forces* 44 (March), 327–341.

Zinn, Howard. (1971) "Marxism and the New Left." Pp. 36–48 in Matthew F. Stolz, ed., *Politics of the New Left*. Beverly Hills, CA: Glencoe.

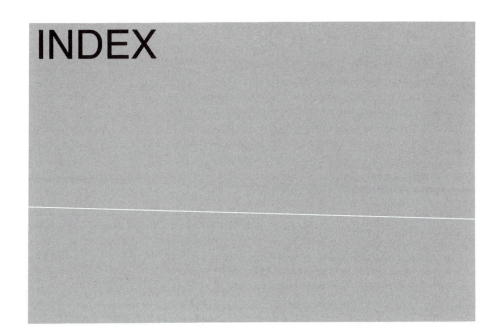

INDEX

A

Access to information, power of, 6
Access to resources, 36–37
Acquiescence with status quo, 4–5
Activism, student, 65–66
Age, cleavages due to, 19, 30
Agenda setting, 79
Alford, Robert R., 5, 69, 70
Alignments, political, 17, 20–32
  biology and parties, 21–22
  everyday life and, 30–32
  historical influences on, 20–21
  in United States, 22–30
Almond, Gabriel A., 27
Althusser, Louis, 5
Ambivalence, sociological, 50–51
Andersen, Kristi, 29
Anderson, John, 39
Anderson, Perry, 72–73
Aristotle, 11
Authority, 7–11, 13, 42
  See also Power, sources of; State, the

B

Badie, Bertrand, 70, 72, 73–74
Banfield, Edward C., 31–32
Barriers to working-class mobilization, 39–41
Beatty, Jack, 45

Belgium, Flemish and Walloons in, 21
Beliefs, 58–59, 60
  See also Ideology(ies)
Bendix, Reinhard, 70
Berelson, Bernard, 23, 62
Biology, social cleavage and, 19–22, 30
Birnbaum, Pierre, 70, 72, 73–74
Black nationalism, 57
Blacks:
  mobilization of in United States, 37–38
  public policy effecting, 80
British Employers Confederation, 75
British Labour Party, 20, 28, 29, 74, 80
Bryan, William Jennings, 22
Bureaucracy, 10, 12–13, 41–43, 72
Burke, Edmund, 53
Burstein, Paul, 46, 80
Business, public policy and power of, 80

C

Canada:
  alignment of Catholics and the Catholic Church in, 26–27
  socialism in, 39–41, 56
Cancian, Francesca M., 5
Capitalism, 72, 78
Carnoy, Martin, 78